From Despair to Hope

A Forty-Day Devotional

SECOND EDITION

Michael W. Langston, PhD, DMin

Kathy J. Langston, PhD

STONE TOWER PRESS

FROM DESPAIR TO HOPE: A Forty-Day Devotional
Copyright © 2017 Michael W. Langston and Kathy J. Langston
All rights reserved.
Revised Edition copyright © 2022

No part of this book may be reproduced in any form or by any electronic or mechanical means including information storage and retrieval systems, without permission in writing from the author. The only exception is by a reviewer, who may quote short excerpts in a review.

Stone Tower Press
7 Ellen Rd.
Middletown, RI 02842
stonetowerpress.com

ISBN: 979-8-9868172-3-1

Formatting and cover design by Amy Cole, JPL Design Solutions

Printed in the United States of America

In this book, as in their first book, *A Journey to Hope*, Michael and Kathy Langston lay bare their experiences as fellow sufferers from the ravages of PTSD and moral injury in the lengthy battle to find healing and peace from the consequences of service to God and country. One thing that this book is not—a pie-in-the-sky, all-will-be-well-with-the-world outlook of a serious battle with trauma and depression. Instead, Mike and Kathy are true spiritual sherpas to guide sufferers as they seek a way out of the depths of suffering to climb to the mountaintop of hope. Waiting on God is a recurring theme as you read biblical passages dealing with the moral injuries of shame, doubt, and disbelief that drag sufferers into the depths of depression, hopelessness, and an alienation from God. Within these pages are meaningful biblical perspectives that impact one's faith. These perspectives and their application in the real world gives spiritual first aid that provides relief to sufferers in their quest to find forgiveness from God, healing of their wounds, acceptance of their hurt, and reconciliation within the faith community. Here you will find a frank acknowledgement of faith's role that leads to a deeper understanding of the ways of God.

Dave DeDonato, Chaplain (LTC), USA Retired
President, South Carolina Chapter, Military Chaplains Association
President, South Carolina Public Safety Chaplains Association

The Bible tells a single story—how God's love secures, safeguards, and sustains us through all our days. The Bible also tells many stories as the living word customizes the one story to each of us to meet us in our deepest need. In *From Despair to Hope*, Mike and Kathy share the story of the Bible in their lives through intimate and vulnerable use of the sacred text to weave a story of hope and healing. Through reading and reflecting on their story, the Lord reveals our own stories to lift each of us from distress to delight. Much more than a devotional, this work comforts, challenges, and guides believers. Making use of broad themes of rescue and redemption from David and Paul, readers claim their own journey of wholeness. An excellent resource for all. *From Despair to Hope* will remain a trusted friend through all times of testing and peace.

Lyman M. Smith
Executive Director
Military Chaplains Association

Trauma, though part and parcel of human life, leads many to retreat into the darkness. Yet, rather than hiding their wounds, the Langstons are fellow pilgrims and experienced guides, using their personal experience as well as historical examples and biblical stories to shine light on our brokenness and lead us on the way to healing. In these forty devotional readings, Mike and Kathy walk with us through the dark night of the soul, leading us from despair to hope. With their meditations and prayers, they give voice to our cries to God, yet they also lead us to reflect on God's faithful character, the only solid basis of hope. I would heartily commend this book to any believer, particularly to those who have experienced trauma!

Brian P. Gault
(PhD, Hebrew-Union College-Jewish Institute of Religion)
Associate Professor of Old Testament and Hebrew,
Columbia Biblical Seminary

This devotional is the perfect companion to the Langstons' popular book, *A Journey to Hope.* While reading as a couple, we found this book to be our friend as we journeyed together through the various themes until we arrived at a place of true peace and hope. We challenge others to find hope through the scriptures, meditations, applications, and prayers contained in the well-written devotional. You will not be disappointed!

Chaplain, Lt Col Brian Bohlman,
Author of *For God and Country: Considering the Call to Military Chaplaincy*

Shelley Bohlman, Military spouse of over 23 years

Individuals and their spouses who live with PTSD will benefit greatly from this devotional work. It intersects the scripture's healing words with PTSD and it's negative effects on relationships. Mike and Kathy's struggles and success with PTSD brings authenticity to this powerful one of a kind devotional book.

Steven E. Keith, D. Min.
Chaplain, (COL), USAF Ret.
Director, Center for Chaplaincy, Liberty University

We dedicate this book to our children
who have stood with us and supported us
as we journeyed with God from despair to hope.

To Michael and Kristin,
Jeff and Heather,
and Elizabeth

Not only that, but we rejoice in our sufferings,
knowing that suffering produces endurance,
and endurance produces character,
and character produces hope,
and hope does not put us to shame,
because God's love has been poured into our hearts
through the Holy Spirit who has been given to us.
Romans 5:3–5 (ESV)

Table of Contents

Foreword

The Chinese philosopher Lao-tzu (604–531 BC) once said, "The journey of a thousand miles begins with a single step." It's an action that requires a measure of risk, courage, and faith.

Taking that first step towards recovery and personal healing from a traumatic experience is the hardest step of all. If you wait for healing to occur from your trauma, most likely, nothing will happen. You have to take the initiative to act decisively and intentionally. Once you take the initial step, other therapeutic measures will suddenly begin to fall into place.

You've just begun a healing journey from traumatic despair to a hopeful future by opening this devotional book. The authors, who vividly shared their own personal experience with the traumatization of war in their book, *A Journey to Hope: Healing the Traumatized Spirit,* have once again created an essential resource for those seeking recovery from traumatic events in their lives.

Readers of this forty-day devotional will find it difficult to stop daily and reflect on the day's inspirational lesson, having the temptation to rush through the chapters dealing with suffering, endurance, and character building to the more pleasant topics of hope and a life void of shame and disappointment. Make a prayerful decision to linger with each daily reading and application if you truly want to experience spiritual growth and healing from a traumatic life experience.

Each devotional begins with a passage from the Holy Bible, powerful God-breathed words that remind us that all of humanity has experienced suffering and loss since Adam and Eve's traumatic expulsion from the presence of God in the Garden of Eden. The relevant biblical passages are followed by a thoughtful devotional reading, a supporting scriptural meditation, a convicting personal application, and an anointed prayerful petition.

As I slowly meditated on each devotional, I was surprised to find myself revisiting some of my own traumatic wounds that I had learned to live with, hidden away with the passage of time. Some of the devotionals are too close to home, leaving you breathless... and without words. Thankfully, the authors lead the reader each day in a thoughtful heartfelt prayer, reminding us of the importance of always directing our pain and suffering to the Father.

Another important experience occurred as I engaged this devotional book. I often thought of family and friends whose lives have been dramatically scarred or altered by traumatic events. I longed to put this book into their hands for their healing and recovery from trauma. You will no doubt come to that same conclusion.

From Despair to Hope is not just another inspirational book to put on your bookshelf. It's an intensely personal, courageous, and candid diary of a faithful Christian couple who disclose their life walk through the "Valley of Baca," demonstrating to the reader that the dryness of our experience with trauma, despair, and hopelessness can become "a place of springs" (Psalm 84:6, ESV) and spiritual renewal. It's a resource that reminds us that all true Christ-followers will "share his sufferings, becoming like him in his death, that by any means possible [we] may attain the resurrection from the dead" (Philippians 3:10–11, ESV). Indeed, this devotional book will help the most damaged soul from trauma to discover that, through our faith in Jesus Christ, we can take each step in the journey of life "from strength to strength" until we see the Author and Finisher of our faith face to face.

MG (CH) Doug Carver, USA, Ret.
Executive Director, Chaplaincy,
North American Mission Board
Southern Baptist Convention

Introduction to the Second Edition

Since our first edition, we have continued to deal with the trauma in our lives. We have re-engaged with this devotional to address the struggles that we continue to have because of the traumatization from war. Our purpose with the Second Edition, however, is to share that Jesus is with us in the broken pieces of our lives. The purpose of this devotional is to walk through a symbolic forty days of moving from disorientation in our relationship to God to reorientation where we understand his presence in our lives in a new and hope-filled way.

We, however, want to be realistic as well. The wounds left by trauma can be triggered by so many happenings outside of our control. Kathy and I have wanted the trauma and its effects to disappear as a result of complete healing. Only traumatization does not work that way with most people. Instead, we have learned to return again and again to the stories of despair, recovery, and hope that are within the Bible and within this book. We continually find our way to God's hope and peace through scripture reading and prayer. The spiritual disciplines bring us in line with God and his will. We have learned to look back on the hard times to find that Jesus was there, and we were not and are not alone.

Dreams, smells, conversations, phrases, and other triggers cause recurrences of the trauma from the combat zone. Waking in the mornings from nights full of Iraq and Afghanistan leave me exhausted physically and emotionally. Over the years, I have found myself discouraged by the fact that the trauma has not healed. I find myself moving into periods of disorientation when I long for the orientation that once was part of my life. I want to feel whole and healed.

Those feelings are my initial ones when I begin to have the nightmares again. I have learned, however, that God is truly in the agony of our lives. I look back at the periods of my life and I can see that Jesus was there in all of those times that I felt alone and in despair. I am learning to fight these periods less and surrender to God more as I journey through my life. I follow the pattern of these devotions in my personal study: reading scripture, focusing on a verse or two, pondering the meaning and application, and then offering a prayer to God. These devotionals mirror my daily devotions as I move through the minefields of dreams and other triggers.

New terminology has emerged in the PTSD/moral injury studies that focuses on the spiritual injuries that traumatized people suffer. The terminology of "spiritual injury" presents a new delineation of trauma for those who are suffering. The guilt, shame, and similar struggles of people with trauma fall within the realm of spiritual injury. The distinctions between moral and spiritual injury leave room for a devotional of this type. Reading scripture, memorizing scripture, and praying are beneficial to all but are especially beneficial to those struggling with the guilt and shame from their traumatic experiences.

We offer an updated second edition with prayers for recovery for those suffering from trauma. We continue to wish you strength for your journey out of the darkness of despair and into the hope that God provides. He invites you to come to him for healing. We encourage you to do so as well. He is in the broken pieces of our lives.

May you find peace through God's love and grace.

Mike and Kathy
Blythewood, SC
20 October 2022

Introduction

If you are hurting, then this book is for you. Your trauma is or was very real. We undertook the writing of this forty-day devotional with the goal of providing a means for those who have been traumatized to find their way from despair to hope. Trauma and its aftermath take over our minds, bodies, and spirits, making it seem impossible to pray, read scripture, or be in relationship with God. Often, the deeper we move into trauma's aftermath, the more distant we feel from God. The struggle to find our way to God often leaves us in despair. Hope seems distant or even impossible. We have written this book to provide a devotional help for these times of darkness and despair. There *is* hope.

This devotional focuses on those suffering from traumatization by war, rape, abuse, or other traumas. Scripture provides many examples of suffering as a way to know God more deeply: Noah and his family endured the destruction of all that was on the earth, Moses and the Israelites wandered in the wilderness, Saul pursued David relentlessly, Jesus fasted and prayed in the wilderness at the beginning of his ministry, a woman who was "unclean" suffered for twelve years, Jesus suffered death on the cross, and many more examples. Thus, through tough times, people in the Bible deepened their relationship with God.

Covering forty days, our devotional revolves around the scripture's use of the number, "40," as a symbol of testing and trials. There are numerous instances of this usage throughout the Bible. During Noah's time, the rains fell for forty days and forty nights to cleanse the earth (Genesis 7:12). The people of Israel wandered in the wilderness for forty years before they could enter the Promised Land (Numbers 32:13, Joshua 5:6). When Jonah arrived in Nineveh, he proclaimed that the people of Nineveh had forty days to repent (Jonah 3:4). Jesus fasted forty days and nights in the wilderness before Satan tested him (Matthew 4:2). Then after his resurrection, Jesus spent forty days on earth before his ascension (Acts 1:3). Many other examples exist within scripture that include forty days or years for periods of time when people are tested and challenged in order to form a deeper relationship with God.

We use the concept of "forty days" as a way to challenge our understanding of traumatic wounds, PTSD, and moral and spiritual injury. Instead of a time of suffering for no reason, we embrace suffering as a time of testing that will lead to new hope and fulfillment—and it is a time that can and will end. When we find ourselves crying out with the Psalmist, "How long, O Lord?" God provides a way for us to move from despair to hope. God is all knowing and is ever present with us. We may feel alone but we are never alone—God is always with us and he knows our suffering. We truly can find comfort in his presence with us and we can always know that he is aware of our struggles. He leads us on the path from despair to hope. Using examples from scripture, from history, and from our lives, we have developed a "road map" for journeying through traumatic injury and despair to find hope through a new and deeper relationship with God.

Using Paul's teachings in Romans 5:3–5, we frame the journey from suffering and despair to hope and peace for those seeking to journey through their wounds to a renewed relationship with God. In Romans 5:3–5, Paul states:

> But we rejoice in our sufferings, knowing that suffering produces endurance, and endurance produces character, and character produces hope, and hope does not put us to shame, because God's love has been

poured into our hearts through the Holy Spirit who has been given to us.

The sections of this devotional align with the stages in Romans 5. Section 1 presents devotionals focused on suffering which include many of David's cries to God in the Psalms. We may not rejoice in our suffering at this time, but with God's help, we can learn to rejoice because of the spiritual path on which suffering places us and the certainty that God is with us as we journey on this path.

Section 2 provides devotionals focused on endurance, since "suffering produces endurance." We must learn to hold on to the truths that we know and learn to endure in our suffering. God is with us and is in the process of forming us into new creations. Section 2 leads readers from endurance and into character. Counter to many Christian teachings of today, we embrace the concept that suffering is a way to deepen our relationship with God. If we endure, then the basic core of who we are—our character—changes in accordance with God's leadership. In that way, we can move deeper into relationship with God and begin to embrace hope.

Section 3 focuses on the ultimate goal: hope. While we have found hope through our Savior, Jesus Christ, we often discover that trauma leads us into despair and we struggle to remember the hope we once had. This section provides ways that God leads us into a new understanding, a new hope. Through this path, the traumatized can find hope for their weary souls. God's hope can remove our shame. Our last section, Section 4, focuses on peace that comes from God pouring his love into our hearts.

On the title page of each section, we have used a quote from Oswald Chambers who wrote the highly-acclaimed devotional *My Utmost for His Highest* (first published in 1924). We chose Chambers because we both have used his powerful devotional over the years. A Scotsman, he grew up as a Baptist and served as a YMCA chaplain to Australian and New Zealand troops (ANZACs) in Egypt during the First World War. Those parallels to our own lives attracted us. Serving as a missionary in Asia and a chaplain to troops in Egypt would have exposed Chambers to many people in traumatic situations. His work focuses on a Christian theology that embraces suffering as a way to deepen our relationship with God. The quotes we have chosen reflect this understanding.

Though our book provides forty days of devotionals, it is not a promise of a "forty day healing process." Healing from trauma, for many people, takes much more time than forty days. Our prayer is that by accepting a forty-day challenge of testing and trials, readers will find themselves launched into a journey that will allow them to move closer and closer to the heart of God.

Each daily devotion presents a scripture reading from the English Standard Version of the Bible. An explanation of the scripture, an historical story, or a personal story follows so that readers can further understand the concepts of suffering and trauma, enduring, character, and hope. A meditation follows in order for readers to spend time focusing on an aspect of the scripture for that day. Memorizing scripture in the Meditation is a way to find comfort throughout the day.

An application allows readers to write out thoughts, fears, or memories that may be blocking them from allowing God to work in their lives. Some applications also challenge readers to move deeper into their relationship with God. Each daily devotion closes with a prayer, which voices the struggles, hurt, and pain that accompany trauma.

The devotions are written from several perspectives. Some of them use our experiences as examples to which readers can relate their own traumatic and life experiences. Some of the devotions present the experiences of warriors, but have broader applications as well. We include stories from the Bible but also from history as examples of people experiencing traumatic injuries. We have used a mixture of approaches so that readers can reflect on the experiences of different people in our time and in the past who have suffered trauma.

Readers may spend forty days moving through this devotional or they may spend unlimited time reflecting on one devotion or in one section. We encourage readers prayerfully to approach each of the devotions, trusting that our God is a God of hope. We can know that God wants us to heal and he wants to lead us again to rejoice in him. He wants to pour his love into our hearts and to fill us with hope and peace.

Jesus suffered extreme trauma on the cross, which was necessary in order for him to provide hope to us through his resurrection. With this example, we can know that God will lead us from the despair that is trauma's aftermath into a new relationship with him that will provide us with hope. God is the provider of hope for us yesterday, today, and tomorrow.

We pray that God will lead you out of despair and into a new life of hope through his love.

Mike and Kathy Langston
Blythewood, SC
August, 2017

DAY 1

The Ultimate Goal

Scripture: Romans 5:3–5

> [3] Not only that, but we rejoice in our sufferings, knowing that suffering produces endurance,[4] and endurance produces character, and character produces hope,[5] and hope does not put us to shame, because God's love has been poured into our hearts through the Holy Spirit who has been given to us.

Devotional Thoughts: "Why me?" is a common cry from Americans when they suffer. Oftentimes, we direct this question at God. We *demand* to know why we are suffering when others apparently are not.

In his letter to the Romans, the Apostle Paul states that we should rejoice in our sufferings. This concept of rejoicing in suffering is not a part of current American culture because we avoid suffering at all costs. When we are forced to suffer, we often complain and resent the experience. Paul, however, teaches that we should rejoice in our suffering.

Suffering is usually a part of traumatic experiences and their aftermaths. As followers of Christ, we are taught in scripture that we are to rejoice in our suffering, that is, to rejoice in our trauma. This statement does not mean that we need to seek traumatic experiences so we can suffer. Instead, scripture teaches of the opportunities we have to grow in our relationship with God through suffering and because of suffering.

Robert Grant, in *The Way of the Wound: A Spirituality of Trauma and Transformation,* defines "trauma" as follows:

> Trauma is not just an event but a constellation of meanings and relationships. Side effects, fears, betrayals, losses of innocence, failures to be understood and the reorganisation of beliefs are all part of the trauma constellation. Trauma demands a change of visions...It activates a profound questioning that differentiates humans from all other forms of life. Trauma is an invitation to change and to pass through the deepest centre of one's nature and come out on the other side. (1996, p. 38)

This invitation to change is what Paul addresses in Romans. As we answer trauma's demand to change our vision, we can learn that suffering produces endurance.

Warriors understand endurance. Intense mental and physical training came before their combat tours. Endurance was the goal in the combat zone because survival was more of a reality if warriors could endure the hardships they faced.

People who endure abuse often focus on survival as well. Those who are traumatized by the tragic loss of loved ones or those who suffer through rape and physical assaults find themselves enduring the traumatic event(s) with a focus on survival. The aftermath of the trauma leaves them struggling to understand God, the world, and life in general. The world, for these traumatic survivors, will never be the same again.

For suffering to produce endurance, we have to avoid despair and hopelessness. That seems an impossible goal; however, with the Holy Spirit's help, we can endure the aftermath of trauma.

From this endurance, we develop character. People who have walked through "the valley of the shadow of death" (Psalm 23:4)—

which for centuries also has been called "the dark night of the soul"—develop depth of character. When such kindred spirits are with us, we learn to focus more on the spiritual aspects of existence and ignore the aspects of our world that are trivial.

Grant explains what the task of those who survive trauma is. He writes:

> The task of every trauma victim is to discover healing and direction in events that not only injure but which have the power to destroy. How to develop hope and spiritual deepening in the midst of despair is a challenge that every survivor must meet. Most humans experience some form of trauma during the course of their lives. Life, in the final analysis, is forever on the verge of overwhelming one's capacities to cope. Traumatic injuries, along with other wounds, are not accidents. They are catalysts that have the potential to place one on the spiritual path. (Grant, 1997, p. 3)

Grant's surprising explanation that traumatic happenings are not accidents, but they can be catalysts—that is, agents of change—to place us on the spiritual path is counter to much of what we often hear or learn about Christianity today. In these traumatic happenings, we are able to develop hope and spiritual deepening. This hope and spiritual deepening germinate in the midst of despair.

Paul, in similar manner, explains that suffering (trauma) leads to endurance. This endurance that causes us to "hang on" in the midst of despair will lead to character. As our character—our core self that contains our spiritual existence—deepens, then we ultimately find hope. The hope we find is in God and his love and forgiveness for us.

Paul continues explaining that this hope will not put us to shame. The shame and guilt that we feel from traumatic experiences dulls in the light of hope that will not put us to shame. We are able to advance through this process from suffering to hope because "God's love has been poured into our hearts through the Holy Spirit who has been given to us." We are assured of God's love for us as we open ourselves to the Holy Spirit to be filled with hope.

Meditation: "God's love has been poured into our hearts." (Romans 5:5b)

Application: Write the steps that Paul lists that take us from suffering to hope. Reread Grant's explanation of trauma and then his explanation of what the tasks of trauma victims are. Commit to allowing the Holy Spirit to guide you to understanding these steps and then applying them to your life so that you move from despair to hope.

Pray for the courage to begin this spiritual journey.

Prayer: Dear God, sometimes the inner pain, the turmoil, and the jumbled up things in my mind are so piercing and agonizing that I just feel like quitting. However, your presence is right beside me. O God, comfort and soothe my soul. It is in that soothing presence that I find solace and an ability to endure and go on. Lead me in the path that you want me to take.

Your presence strengthens me, providing me with the ability to go on. For that, I will praise you forever. You provide me with the ability to walk through the dark night of the soul to a place of healing. In you, my Lord, I find hope that quiets and restores my hurting soul. Now I sing praises to your glorious name, the name that heals and gives hope, the name of Jesus who is my Lord forever. Amen.

SECTION 1

Suffering Produces Endurance

"No healthy Christian ever chooses suffering;
he chooses God's will, as Jesus did,
whether it means suffering or not."
—*Oswald Chambers*

DAY 2

Refusing Comfort

Scripture: Psalm 77:1–3

> 1 I cry aloud to God,
> aloud to God, and he will hear me.
> 2 In the day of my trouble, I seek the Lord;
> in the night, my hand is stretched out without wearying;
> my soul refuses to be comforted.
> 3 When I remember God, I moan;
> when I meditate, my spirit faints.

Devotional Thoughts: From 2005 through 2008, I spent twenty-four of thirty months in combat zones, first in Afghanistan (eleven months) and then in Fallujah, Iraq (fourteen months). Almost every moment I was in Afghanistan, I thought about leaving that country and returning home. My six-month Afghan deployment extended to eleven months, but I knew I would return home.

When I did return, technically, the five months that I spent at home before I went to Fallujah, Iraq, were spent preparing for war again. I was home; yet, I was focused on my next combat tour and never really felt "at home."

I spent the next fourteen months in Iraq, and the days, weeks, and months slowly ticked away. My focus grew more and more on returning home. I knew that if I just got home, then the chaos of the combat zone, the putrid smells that surrounded me, and the terrors that lurked everywhere would end. I would be safe and I would again worship well.

When I returned home at the end of these thirty months, however, I was unable to turn off my hypervigilent approach to survival. As the weeks passed, I realized that chaos and terror had followed me home. I cried out to God for help, but I felt so removed from him. Verse 2 says, "My soul refuses to be comforted." My initial response to this verse was that I have always been open to comfort from God. After all, I spent my career as a chaplain who taught the truths of scripture to people. In my days of trouble, I had always sought God and he had responded.

Yet, I found myself deeper and deeper in darkness. I remembered God, but my soul refused to be comforted. When I would pray and meditate on scripture, my spirit would be numbed ("faint," v. 3). I found myself with no words, just moaning before God. Yet, I saw no way out of the chaos in my mind and pain in my spirit.

Trauma can push us deeper and deeper into darkness. Our dreams are filled with images and horrors that haunt us when daylight comes. Prayer is empty and scripture no longer has meaning. We find ourselves filled with fear and loneliness. The dreams that haunt our nights and days, the flashbacks, and the fears of the unknown force us to protect what is left of our souls. We often find ourselves unable to be open because of our fear. We struggle to hear God. We are unable to feel his presence. We numb our spirits to protect us from the chaos.

When we are traumatized, we often develop a protective mode to prevent further pain. That protective mode, however, traps our spirit and prevents us from experiencing the comfort, healing, and care that God provides through his Holy Spirit. When we live a life of fear and self-protection in trauma's aftermath, then God can seem distant and uncaring. Our cries to him seem to be unheard. Our isolation from God and from people seems complete. We must, as the Psalmist often mentions, remember the times that God was with us.

God remains present with us in these times and in all times. He cares for us and knows what we fear. God will come to us and comfort us through these times if we can learn to open ourselves again to his care.

Meditation: "My soul refuses to be comforted." (Psalm 77:2b)

Application: In your quiet time, examine your protective mode. Think of your responses to situations. Are you responding from a self-protective mode that prevents you from experiencing God?

Pray that God will show you the way toward opening your spirit to his care.

Prayer: Eternal Father in heaven, I call out to you with all my being. O how I desire to hear your voice, your refreshing and life giving voice. Day after day I feel as if I am so tense, keyed up, and on edge. It is as if I have to constantly protect myself—even from you, O Lord.

Where are you, my Father in heaven? Where is your healing balm that soothes my soul? I cry out to you and it seems that you do not hear my cries and pleas for help. But I remember your presence lives within me through your Holy Spirit.

Cause me to be still and to listen for your voice. As you speak to me, Lord, help me to hear you and to be refreshed by your words of life. As I walk through the dark valleys of my experiences, be forever with me. Be my courage, my strength, and my guide. I know I am not alone, O God. You are my peace, an ever-present help in times of despair. In you, I trust; in you, I find my hope. Thank you for showing me the way forward, O Lord my God. In your wonderful and holy name I pray. Amen.

DAY 3

Spiritual Injury

Scripture: Psalm 25:6–7, 11, 16

> 6 Remember your mercy, O Lord, and your steadfast love,
> for they have been from of old.
> 7 Remember not the sins of my youth or my transgressions;
> according to your steadfast love remember me,
> for the sake of your goodness, O Lord!
> 11 For your name's sake, O Lord,
> pardon my guilt, for it is great.
> 16 Turn to me and be gracious to me,
> for I am lonely and afflicted.

Devotional Thoughts: Posttraumatic Stress Disorder. PTSD. Spiritual injury. Posttraumatic growth. Depression. Mental illness. Moral injury. Physical illness. Guilt. Shame. Nightmares. Flashbacks. It has all been defined and discussed with everyone seeking the right name that encapsulates all that is within the mind, body, and spirit of those traumatized by war, physical abuse, loss of limbs, and other traumatic experiences.

We seek to be free of the guilt and shame that have become the filter for all events in our lives. We need relief. We need to be forgiven.

David prays for God to extend his mercy and steadfast love to David as he struggles with guilt and shame. He begs God to forget the sins of his youth. David pleads for God to remember him. David, the man after God's own heart, struggled to be free of the guilt and shame of his experiences in the same way that we do.

Asking God to pardon his guilt, David confesses that the guilt is too great for him to bear. David then asks God to turn to him and be gracious. David's longing for reprieve from his guilt and shame overshadows his life. He turns to God to ask for forgiveness for deeds that are not mentioned in this passage.

The last section of David's confession reveals that David, King of Israel, was lonely and afflicted. The guilt and shame David bore separated him from the people around him. David felt outside of normal society. He was lonely and he felt great pain and suffering (affliction). In the words of Walter Brueggemann (2002), David was experiencing a time of "disorientation" and chaos (p. x). David felt disoriented from God, from those near him, and from the world around him.

"Spiritual injury" has become a current way of identifying what David is expressing. Warriors returning from war have to deal with the guilt and shame that comes from actions they saw or participated in or possibly from actions they felt they should have done (such as somehow keeping a buddy alive). The guilt and shame can lead to depression and suicide. The spiritual injuries of war affect the deep self that David refers to in this Psalm. Thus, spiritual injury can be the result of periods of overwhelming disorientation.

Those of us who have suffered sexual, physical, or mental abuse experience spiritual injury as well. Our shame and guilt, our feelings of unworthiness, and our continual questioning of our traumatic experiences (Why did I choose that way home? What if I had done something differently? Why didn't I fight back?) also lead to depression and suicide. Our core spiritual self is damaged by trauma. We, like David, seek forgiveness and acceptance by a community of God. We seek wholeness for our wounded spiritual selves.

David describes his own spiritual injury in this passage. He turns to God, asking God to forgive him and to forget the sins of the past. In like manner, we can turn to God for forgiveness no matter how guilty and full of shame we are. We can also ask God to forget the sins that we have committed.

But how do we know that God forgives us? How do we free ourselves from the guilt and shame of things we have done or things we have left undone? How can God forgive us for these things? How can we move through these periods of disorientation and find a new orientation to God and the world around us?

God acknowledges that we sin and that we do not live perfect lives. We know that he acknowledges this because he sent his Son, Jesus, to die in our place. Jesus died for our sins so that we can ask for forgiveness and receive it…no matter what we have done.

David also knew that God would forgive him. David had experienced God's forgiveness earlier in his life and he knew of the forgiving power that God had shown Israel through history. David reassures us of this forgiveness in Psalm 32:5 when he says that he confessed his sin to God and that God has forgiven the sin.

A beginning step of moving out of periods of disorientation is to turn and face those things that cause us shame and guilt. Facing them allows us to confess them. Confessing them allows us to experience God's forgiveness. Through the forgiveness, we then can begin—with the Holy Spirit's help—to find our way into a new orientation to God and his work in our lives.

We must turn and walk through the dark night of the soul—the spiritual injury itself. We have to face the injury and walk through it in order to reach the light on the other side. This light is our *hope,* found through the guiding presence of the Holy Spirit leading us to healing, forgiveness, and re-orientation as we are renewed through *faith.*

We are assured of forgiveness and of freedom from our sin. We are assured of God's help as we struggle with spiritual injury. God assures us of his forgiveness as well as his desire for us to be in a deeper relationship with him.

Meditation: "O LORD, pardon my guilt, for it is great." (Psalm 25:11b)

Application: Make a list of the items that cause you guilt and shame. This list is a difficult list. One by one, go down the list, using the prayer below. Insert each item as you pray.

Prayer: O God...I acknowledge my sin to you. I am not covering my iniquity. I confess the following: ____________. I ask your forgiveness for this. Cleanse me and help me to know and experience the removal of my guilt and shame.

I have said to you, "I confess my transgressions to the Lord," and you have forgiven the iniquity of my sin (Psalm 32:5). Hear my prayer, O Lord. Let me feel your cleansing Spirit. Move through my being as you heal my wounded and traumatized spirit. Let me find rest and forgiveness through you. This is my prayer and petition, O Lord my God. Amen.

DAY 4

Chaos to Order

Scripture: Genesis 1:1–2, 31

> [1] In the beginning, God created the heavens and the
> earth. [2] The earth was without form and void, and dark-
> ness was over the face of the deep. And the Spirit of God
> was hovering over the face of the waters.... [31] And God
> saw everything that he had made, and behold, it was
> very good. And there was evening and there was morn-
> ing, the sixth day.

Devotional Thoughts: Rain had fallen for almost three weeks, saturating the ground in the midlands and coastal regions of South Carolina. Then three weather systems converged and stalled over an area from Columbia to the coast. Heavy rains, starting on Friday, fell for hours and then days, setting records for twenty-four hour periods.

In the early morning hours on Sunday, an obscure earthen dam in the northeast part of Columbia breached, no longer able to hold back the water pouring into the lake. As the dam cracked and then broke, water poured through the collapsed dam, rushing down Jackson Creek. This water flooded into the next lake, which caused that lake's dam to break. The wall of water released from this breached dam rushed downstream to cause another dam to breach. The reaction continued downstream as earthen dam after earthen dam breached with water rising rapidly and spreading throughout sections of Columbia that had never before flooded.

People throughout Columbia woke to find water rising rapidly in their houses. Peering out their windows into the dark, they could make out cars floating down the streets accompanied by other items from yards, garages, and homes. Grabbing children and pets, people tried to open their front doors only to find that water several feet deep rushed into their homes. Up was the only direction people could go as the water rose rapidly. In the dark hours of Sunday morning, apartment building and house roofs throughout many neighborhoods were crowded with people seeking safety from the chaos below.

Proximity. Intensity. Duration (Meadors & Lamson 2008). These three storms stall over trauma victims to produce chaos within their minds, bodies, and spirits. When the pressures from the proximity to horror and terror breaches the spirit to combine with the intensity of experiences, which then crash into the duration of exposure to traumatic events, the entirety of the mind, body, and spirit are flooded with the chaos of terror and horrors. Oftentimes, traumatic survivors then live in the chaos which floods into their minds, bodies, and spirits. This can result in post-traumatic stress and moral and spiritual injury. These traumatic survivors, like the flood victims, often watch as what they treasure the most in life floats away while they seek safety from the storms that continually assault them.

The passage from Genesis describes the chaos that existed before God began his work. In this chaos, the Spirit of God hovered over the face of the waters. God created the heavens and the earth, and *then* he shaped the heavens and earth and all that was on the earth. From the chaos, God created everything that exists and all of it was good. God is all powerful. God can turn chaos into goodness, despair into hope.

From the chaos in our minds, bodies, and spirits, God can create newness and goodness within us. The path, however, is a journey through our spirits to the heart of God. To begin this journey, we must remember who God is. He is all-powerful and all-knowing. Most of all, he cares deeply for us and desires to have us journey into his love that offers hope and peace for our weary souls.

In the midst of the chaos in your spirit, realize that the Spirit of God is hovering over you. God will work to form a new creation from the chaos in your mind and spirit. You are not alone and you are not unprotected. God is with you and the Holy Spirit hovers over you.

Just as the flood victims moved up to rooftops in order to be safe from the floodwaters, you can also move "up" to find safety from the chaos in your spirit. Trust God to bring you out of the storms and chaos of your life. Believe that he will take this trauma and make something good from it.

Meditation: "And God saw everything that he had made, and behold, it was very good." (Genesis 1:31)

Application: Make a list of the storms in your life that seem to be stalled over you. As you look at this list, pray that God will help you find your way out of the chaos and into his safety. Ask him to be present with you and to help you understand that he is protecting you.

Begin each morning with a prayer that acknowledges that God is present with you. Repeat that prayer throughout the day.

Prayer: I pray that you would come and stand with me, O God. Come and hover over me, be my shelter, and be my liberator from the turmoil that encircles me. Give me the ability to move to higher ground and bask in the safety and security that your presence provides.

In your presence, O Lord, my soul is lifted up and new life springs forth. Because of your faithfulness to me, as part of your people, I am renewed and my life has new meaning. Be my ever-present help as I step forward with the knowledge and surety of your blessing and presence in my life. Restore my health, my sanity, and my physical abilities to be the vibrant person you have created me to be. This I pray in the most holy name of your Son, Jesus Christ, my Lord. Amen

DAY 5

Belonging

Scripture: Ephesians 3:14–19

> 14 For this reason I bow my knees before the Father, 15 from whom every family in heaven and on earth is named, 16 that according to the riches of his glory he may grant you to be strengthened with power through his Spirit in your inner being, 17 so that Christ may dwell in your hearts through faith—that you, being rooted and grounded in love, 18 may have strength to comprehend with all the saints what is the breadth and length and height and depth, 19 and to know the love of Christ that surpasses knowledge, that you may be filled with all the fullness of God.

Devotional Thoughts: Too often, warriors feel that they no longer belong in the places they lived, worked, and worshipped before they spent time in a combat zone. The traumatizing experiences in the combat zone change warriors for the rest of their lives.

Many years ago, we lived in the mountains of North Carolina where I pastored a church. The church members were mainly older (70s and 80s). The idea of their church as a family was a deeply held feeling among the members of the church. They cared for each other and accepted each other unconditionally. As a young pastor, I had many ideas for changing this church.

The church members, while caring deeply for each other, did not embrace change very well. At first, I was stunned at their resistance to embracing new people in their congregation. But I came to understand how God shapes church families so that they provide care that strengthens members in the trials, deaths, traumas, and hardships of life.

The members of the church seemed to be overly protective of some of the members. One man, in particular, would scream at business meetings and other times that we discussed changing the way they did church. After one highly charged confrontation, church members followed the man out the door to provide comfort to him.

Other church members came up to us and said, "You will have to excuse him. He was in the war, you know. He used to be the kindest man, but the war changed all that."

At the time, I was shocked that this man was exploding with so much anger forty years after World War II. But in hindsight, the love of this church family that had supported this man through his forty-year struggle amazed us. God had provided those church members with the power to strengthen this man as he fought the decades long battle with the chaos in his mind.

Finding a church that can support us as we seek to be strengthened by the Holy Spirit can be a challenge. God, however, will provide the strength we need through his riches in glory and through those who care about our wounds. We have to be courageous as we seek that church family. Some churches attempt to support the traumatized, but from lack of understanding, they miss the mark. Our best intentions do not always provide us with the understanding we need to minister to the hidden wounds of the traumatized. God, however, has provided church communities that will support the traumatized returning from war.

As returning warriors, we have the need to fit into a church community. While there are churches and people who are not accepting, there are many more that are. We know that we are members of God's family and he accepts us with our wounds, guilt, and sin. He forgives us and loves us. In some cases, we must educate people in churches on how to accept wounded warriors.

God strengthens us through his Spirit and he fills us with love and hope. He assures us of his acceptance. As members of his family, we are rooted and grounded in his love. Along with the other family members, we can know the endless love of God.

Like the man in my church, we can be surrounded by members of God's family who will care for us and accept us in times of need. God sends his Holy Spirit to fill us and minister to us when we have flashbacks and nightmares.

God promises that we will "know the love of Christ that surpasses knowledge," and that we will "be filled with all the fullness of God." He cares for us and we remain members of God's family. Keep the faith and trust that God will provide you with a church family that strengthens you.

Meditation: "That according to the riches of his glory he may grant you to be strengthened with power through his Spirit in your inner being." (Ephesians 3:16)

Application: Think of some incidents when you responded in ways that were not "socially acceptable." How would you have felt if friends had surrounded you and guided you toward calmness? Write those feelings down.

Pray that God will let you feel that you are a member of his family. Begin to tell yourself that you DO belong—you belong in God's family.

Prayer: O Father in heaven, how good and comforting it is to be wrapped in the warmth and glory of your love. This love comes from being understood, forgiven, and accepted as your very own. At times the traumatic memories invade our minds and destroy our knowledge of your love. The memories threaten us with change that is scary and overwhelming. But you provide a love that surpasses knowledge and knowing.

You make your love a reality in our lives as we place ourselves totally in your hands. Your peace is an abiding peace that fills us with the goodness of your Divine Being. We experience your unfailing and healing love that brings peace to our damaged souls.

Thank you, Lord, for the healing and hope that you bring into our lives. Thank you also for your peace. In the Name of the Christ who came to change the world to your glory. Amen.

DAY 6

Displacement from Our Lives

Scripture: Romans 12:1–2

> [1] I appeal to you therefore, brothers, by the mercies of God, to present your bodies as a living sacrifice, holy and acceptable to God, which is your spiritual worship.
> [2] Do not be conformed to this world, but be transformed by the renewal of your mind, that by testing you may discern what is the will of God, what is good and acceptable and perfect.

Devotional Thoughts: In the latter part of October 2015, several days of rain followed the initial breaches of many of the earthen dams in Columbia, SC. During those days, water flowing downstream caused most of the dams to breach. Finally, however, the rains ceased and the waters receded. People returned to homes that had had six feet or more of filthy water flowing through them. Many people returned to shells of homes because most of their belongings had washed away.

Columbia's high humidity did nothing to help preserve what was left of people's household goods. Mold and mildew filled every space that the water left. Shells of homes filled with moldy furniture greeted people as they returned home. The floods had washed away memories, dirtied cherished items, and ruined treasured possessions. In the course of several days, people lost that which they thought was permanent. The clean up would take weeks and months, but nothing would ever be the same. Though temporary shelters provided for people's immediate needs, no shelter could provide for the displacement from their previous lives that the flood victims suffered.

Walter Brueggemann describes a "transformed faith" that is in opposition to most current approaches to God and church. This transformed faith responds to a God "who is present in, participating in, and attentive to the darkness, weakness, and displacement of life. The God addressed in these does not *conform*" (2002, p. 27).

Trauma results from experiencing and participating in some of the darkest parts of humanity. The terrors of the trauma whether experienced in a combat zone, on a roof with rising waters, during a sexual assault, in a catastrophic auto accident, or in other areas of life follow people in their daily lives and fill their nightmares. Traumatized individuals often have their physical bodies seemingly free of trauma; yet, their minds and spirits remain in the horrors of the happenings that they experienced. People are deeply transformed by traumatic happenings.

Traumatized individuals often find themselves displaced from the life they knew before the traumatic happenings. Traumatized people struggle to find God in most of our churches where people worship a God that appears only in the orderly parts of their lives. God, however, comes to us in all happenings of our lives—orderly and chaotic.

People who are transformed by their traumatic experiences have an opportunity to find renewal in their minds through our God who is present with us in the chaos in our minds, who is participating in the horrors that fill our spirits, and who is attentive to the darkness in our souls. He is with us as we realize how displaced we are from our previous lives. God provides a way for us that leads us to what is "good and acceptable and perfect."

Meditation: "Be transformed by the renewal of your mind." (Romans 12:2b)

Application: As you pray today, ask God to show you his presence in the midst of your chaos. As you continue through your day, ponder God's presence in your life during the times of chaos and confusion. Record the places where he was with you and you were unaware of his presence.

Prayer: Eternal Father, you are indeed from everlasting to everlasting and are sovereign over all things in creation, especially our lives. The proximity, intensity, and duration to traumatic events has left me in chaos. Even in the midst of this chaos, your presence, O God, stills the turmoil and disorder that floods my body, mind, and spirit.

Be present in my life right now and calm the raging storms within me. Be present and remove the pressures of unspeakable horrors that continuously flood my mind. Be present, O Lord, and touch my spirit with your undergirding hand of calmness, comfort, and care that heals my whole being. Cause me to know, Heavenly Father, that in you and you alone, I can find peace and healing.

Now I pray that you would graciously provide me with the strength and courage to walk steadfastly into this day knowing you are with me and that you are my rock and my salvation. To God be the glory, honor, and praise now and forevermore. Amen.

DAY 7

Forgotten by God

Scripture: Psalm 13:1–6

> 1 How long, O LORD? Will you forget me forever?
> How long will you hide your face from me?
> 2 How long must I take counsel in my soul
> and have sorrow in my heart all the day?
> How long shall my enemy be exalted over me?
> 3 Consider and answer me, O LORD my God;
> light up my eyes, lest I sleep the sleep of death,
> 4 lest my enemy say, "I have prevailed over him,"
> lest my foes rejoice because I am shaken.
> 5 But I have trusted in your steadfast love;
> my heart shall rejoice in your salvation.
> 6 I will sing to the LORD,
> because he has dealt bountifully with me.

Devotional Thoughts: In late 1996, we began our four-year assignment in Iceland. Our first winter in Iceland changed our appreciation of the sun. We arrived in October, just as the amount of light and the amount of dark were equal. Then slowly, the sun rose later and later in the morning. It set earlier each day. Darkness lasted longer and longer.

The shortest day of the year saw the sun rise around 11:30 am and set around 2:30 pm. The other twenty-one hours of the day were filled with darkness. We could only see lights around the bay, which seemed very distant. Mountains, lava fields, and oceans were lost in the darkness.

Our first year was the most difficult. The dark consumed everything for so many hours of the day. Day after day, we waited for the light to be there when we woke up and stay until dinner-time. The dark seemed to last forever.

As time passed, the days became longer and the nights become shorter. In retrospect, the darkness of the first winter did not last as long as it seemed to. The next three winters were filled with more hope since we had experienced the ending of darkness. We knew it would end. Our first winter, however, was a dark one.

King David, in this Psalm, is experiencing a dark time. He questions God with "How long?" He asks why God has forgotten him and how long will God continue to hide his face. God welcomes these questions and we can ask with David, "How long will this last?" and "Where are you?"

David knows that God has not forgotten him; yet, David *feels* as though God has turned his back. David struggles spiritually to feel the presence of God.

When we enter the darkness that is sexual abuse, extreme loss, war, emotional abuse, etc., we often cease to feel God's presence in our lives. Darkness seems to consume us. We struggle to feel the presence of God when we are reeling from trauma. The questions of "How long?" and "Why?" are the cries of the traumatized. We stumble around in darkness, unsure of where we are. Darkness, pain, and chaos encompass our lives. We question whether this darkness will ever end.

God draws us to him, however. Just as the second winter was easier in Iceland, we know that God will comfort us and he will be present with us. David ends his Psalm with this knowledge. Remembering what God has done for him in the past, David embraces those memories for confidence in God. He knows that the darkness will end.

Meditation: "How long, O LORD? Will you forget me forever?" (Psalm 13:1)

Application: The Psalms provide a prayer language for us. When we lift our cries of "How long?" and "Why?" to God, he responds to us.

Write a prayer that shares the pain you are experiencing. Use the words of Psalm 13 or use words of your own. Pray this prayer for a week.

Under this prayer, write one experience that you have had where God provided for you. Once you have finished your prayer, thank God for his provision during that time.

Prayer: O Jesus, you are my Lord and my peace. When my spirit is downcast and the sky above me is filled with dark clouds, you are always there. In this time of doubt, hurt, and pain come alongside me and weigh me down.

Cause me to stand straight and to have a certainty that your arms are wrapped around me. Protect me and give me a sense of refuge in which I can find solace and a restored spirit. I lift up my countenance unto you, O Lord. I lift up my being and place all that I am and all that I have in your care. Help me know to be still and to know that you are my God and are an ever present help in times of trouble. In your holy name which is exalted highly and elevated above all the mountains, I pray. Amen.

DAY 8

Home as a Foreign Country

Scripture: Luke 5:12–13

> 12 While [Jesus] was in one of the cities, there came a
> man full of leprosy. And when he saw Jesus, he fell on
> his face and begged him, "Lord, if you will, you can
> make me clean." 13 And Jesus stretched out his hand and
> touched him, saying, "I will; be clean." And immediately
> the leprosy left him.

Devotional Thoughts: In his book, *The Go-Between,* L. P. Heartly states, "The past is a foreign country. They do things differently there." This statement pinpoints a major problem for service members returning from combat zones—they no longer remember who they were before they left for war.

The problems for service members and others who are traumatized arise when family members and friends who remember the persons that service members used to be now expect them to be the same as they were before the deployment. Only the past is no longer recognizable to warriors and they do not know how to respond. The past is a foreign country where they do things differently.

War changes the core of people who experience it. Would we really want people to smell the smells, taste the tastes, see the horrors, and hear the sounds of war and not be changed? This change is the essence of moral and spiritual injury.

Before the unit leaves for combat zones, the unit moves into an up-tempo pace that involves work days that last eighteen hours, advanced training, advanced certifications to meet mission requirements, higher stress, a series of training packages tailored to specific military missions, heightened alertness as well as other training and drills that are meant to fine-tune the actions of the unit and the ship. During up-tempo times, the expectations are high and the stress is intensified.

Upon putting their own boots on the ground, warriors enter an enhanced reality that cannot be equaled in any other life experience. They begin living at an up-tempo pace that lasts for their tour of three, four, six, twelve, or fourteen months. The up-tempo pace that is within the combat zone takes on a heightened sense of purpose. Lives depend on split second decisions and on split second reactions. Over and over the military drills reactions into men and women so that when they are under attack, they will respond according to their training.

In discussing problems that warriors experience in and after leaving the combat zone, Charles Hoge notes the following:

> During times of stress and danger, the body is revved up due to adrenaline and other chemicals; the heart rate is increased, breathing becomes more rapid and shallow, muscle tension increases, and the mind becomes hyperalert. As a result, warriors are able to maintain high situational awareness, which is a very useful skill. This includes scanning the environment for anything that might be a threat, using their own fear or anxiety as a warning signal, and ensuring that there are always escape routes. (2010, p. 58)

Warriors live in this intensity for their tour of duty. When they return home, the pace is slower and the danger is lessened;

however, warriors may not be able to move out of that up-tempo pace. They return home constantly hyperalert with no real memory of any other way to act.

The people at home, however, are keenly aware of the differences. This awareness leads warriors to feel that they are outsiders and that they no longer belong anywhere. Many people at home begin to avoid warriors because of the intensity of their actions. Other people who have been changed by traumatic experiences know these same feelings of being outsiders who no longer belong.

In Jesus' day, lepers were the outcasts of society. Leprosy was a disease that had no cure but was highly contagious. Those who developed the disease were forced out of their homes and towns. They lived alone near the cities and towns, but not in them. Laws forbade the lepers from approaching people and the lepers could never touch another person because they could spread the disease.

In the scripture from Luke, a leper ignored all of the social restrictions and the religious restrictions. He ran out to greet Jesus, falling on his face as he asked Jesus to heal him. Jesus agreed and healed the man so that all the leprosy was gone. Jesus spoke and the leper was healed.

Jesus' openness to the leper shows us that Jesus welcomes us when society, families, and religious institutions do not welcome us. Lepers had physical ailments that caused them to be outcasts from all parts of society. Warriors and others who are traumatized have spiritual wounds that cause them to be outcasts in their families and in their churches.

This scripture passage proves that Jesus accepts us, even if those around us reject us. With Jesus, we do not have to struggle to remember who we were. When the past feels like a foreign country where they do things differently, we can know that Jesus embraces us as his family. We can do things differently and Jesus still accepts us. He accepts us if we are hyperalert with no memory of another way to live. Jesus gives us a new life in him.

Jesus provides us with peace and with healing when we turn to him with our pain and rejection. Trust that Jesus will heal your spiritual wound—your moral injury—just as he did the leper.

Meditation: "Jesus stretched out his hand and touched him, saying, 'I will; be clean.'" (Luke 5:13b)

Application: Pray that Jesus will heal your spirit and teach you his ways. Share the pain of isolation that you feel. Pray that his peace will fill your spirit today.

Prayer: Sometimes Lord, the intensity is so great inside me that I can hardly function. Adrenalin races through me. I feel so out of sorts that I can hardly sit still. My mind races and everything around me picks up speed. Sometimes I wonder if I am really here experiencing all of this. It is almost like being back on the battlefield and it scares the heck out of me.

Calm my spirit, O Lord. Cleanse and heal my fragmented emotions. Calm my being and give me a sense of safety so that I can slow down and experience your presence in my life. Take away that feeling of constant alertness. May your peace be the balm that soothes my soul and fills me with peace. Comfort me, O God, and help me trust in you with all my being. So I will praise your name forever, Lord God, and may your radiance be the glory of all heaven now and forever. Amen.

DAY 9

Where Is Your Faith?

Scripture: Psalm 27:9–14

9 Hide not your face from me.
Turn not your servant away in anger,
O you who have been my help.
Cast me not off; forsake me not,
O God of my salvation!
10 For my father and my mother have forsaken me,
but the LORD will take me in.
11 Teach me your way,
O LORD, and lead me on a level path
because of my enemies.
12 Give me not up to the will of my adversaries;
for false witnesses have risen against me,
and they breathe out violence.
13 I believe that I shall look upon the goodness of the LORD
in the land of the living!
14 Wait for the LORD;
be strong, and let your heart take courage;
wait for the LORD!

Devotional Thoughts: The beginning of this Psalm by King David is an often-quoted passage. "The Lord is my light and my salvation;

whom shall I fear? The Lord is the stronghold of my life; of whom shall I be afraid?" (Psalm 27:1). David's strong statements of fearlessness center on the Lord God's protection of him.

In verse 5, David exclaims, "For he will hide me in his shelter in the day of trouble; he will conceal me under the cover of his tent; he will lift me high upon a rock." David is confident of God's protection. God will provide whatever is needed to protect David.

We often consider this approach to God as "normal" life. When we are in a "normal" cycle of life, we are confident in God's protection. We are safe within his care. Nothing will harm us because God will protect us. This time is a period of orientation when all is right with our world.

Yet, trauma strikes in our lives and often, our first question is "Why is God letting this happen to me?" Beginning in verse 9, David feels that God is distant and cannot be found. The God of his salvation has cast David off, leaving him to his enemies. David cries out to God that even his mother and father have forsaken him, leaving him alone. Feeling alienated from God, family, and friends, David pleads with God to lead him on a level path. People accuse David of actions that are false. He has nowhere to turn and is overwhelmed by his isolation and aloneness. David has entered a period of disorientation.

David suffered from many traumatic instances in his life. This Psalm takes us through the cycle of his life where David goes from "up" to "down." The message in this Psalm is how David copes with his alienation from God, family, and friends. When he is at a low point, David still cries out to God, expressing his alienation and his despair.

Stating that God has, in the past, always been faithful, David speaks words of reassurance. He does not recommend instant relief. Instead, David's Psalm calls on us to bring our despair and lost hopes to God. David pours his heart out to God. Then David reminds us to wait on the Lord and remember what God has done for us in the past. God will lead us into a new orientation where we can have a deeper relationship with him.

David's closing words are of hope and courage. He states that he will again "look upon the goodness of the Lord," and then he twice encourages us to wait on the Lord. We tend to be an impatient people. God, however, has infinite patience. We demand hope and he tells us to wait as he grows us into new people.

Waiting for God is a difficult practice, especially as we deal with the fears, alienation, and horrors of traumatic experiences. Hope, however, can be found by waiting on the Lord. God will reorient us if we wait on him.

Meditation: "Be strong, and let your heart take courage; wait for the LORD!" (Psalm 27:14b)

Application: Write down ten ways that God has worked in your life. Read over that list and thank God for these blessings. Then write down five ways that you feel alienated from those around you. Read over that list as a prayer to God. Reaffirm your faith that he will work good in your life. Ask God to help you wait on him.

Prayer: Lord, everything is in disarray. I feel like everyone is against me and no one understands what I am experiencing. I even wonder where you are in the midst of all these feelings.

Are my enemies real? Am I crazy? Did these things really happen to me? Am I really damaged goods? Father, it surely feels that way. But I know you are my strength and a place where I can find refuge. O help me to experience that refuge more often in the daily living of my life.

Lord, you are indeed faithful and always present, even when I cannot see, hear, or feel you. In those times, be my hope and cause me to wait upon you. Help me be still and patient as you work out the groanings of my life. For I know you are indeed good and caring, O God. Therefore, I will wait upon your presence as I reaffirm my faith in you. Wrap me in your arms and cause me to trust in you all the more. Thank you, Lord. In the name of the most High, the ever loving God of all eternity, I pray. Amen.

DAY 10

Abandoned by God

Scripture: Psalm 22:1–2

> 1 My God, my God, why have you forsaken me?
> Why are you so far from saving me, from the words of my groaning?
> 2 O my God, I cry by day, but you do not answer,
> and by night, but I find no rest.

Mark 15:34

> 34 And at the ninth hour Jesus cried with a loud voice, "*Eloi, Eloi, lema sabachthani?*" which means, "My God, my God, why have you forsaken me?"

Devotional Thoughts: Happy face Christianity says that if we love God enough and have enough faith, then nothing will ever go wrong in our lives. When something does go wrong—seriously wrong—then the simplistic answer is that we do not have enough faith.

The results of suffering from traumatic events can be a questioning of our beliefs. We move from a period of orientation (pretrauma) to disorientation (during and after the traumatic event).

What we believed about God, his presence, and his love no longer fits with what we know about life.

Robert Grant points to this time—the time of disorientation—as the time where the Holy Spirit can reach us in the modern world. Happy face Christianity does not embrace trauma as a way to God (Grant, 1996); yet, David and Jesus suffered periods of disorientation.

David, who God called a man after God's own heart, experienced times when he felt abandoned by God. This Psalm asks why God has forsaken (abandoned) David. No answer comes from God when David cries out to him by day. At night, David finds no rest. David asks why God is so far from saving him, from rescuing him from the terrors that fill David's mind.

Jesus, God's Son, asks the same question as he hangs on the cross. Jesus cries out to God, asking why God has abandoned him. In the midst of the agony of the cross, Jesus feels separated from God.

Jesus and David were closer to God than most humans; yet, they both experienced extreme trauma and feelings of being abandoned by God. Thus, the modern explanation of needing "more faith" does not fit with our Biblical role models.

When they were suffering tremendously, both Jesus and David cried out to God for relief. That example is one that we should follow. When we are suffering from the after-effects of trauma, including questioning where God is, we should direct our questioning to God. He welcomes our complaints.

Turning to God in our times of agony means that we trust him to help us even when we cannot feel his presence. He will help us but not necessarily immediately and not in the way we *want.* God provides for us in the way that we *need.*

David's agony ceased and he became king of Israel. Jesus' agony ceased with his death. Jesus, however, conquered death and through his agony, we have eternal life. Without the agony of the cross, we would not have the hope of the resurrection.

God welcomes the relationship that comes from sharing our suffering. Know that if you feel abandoned by God, he is still there. Trust him for deliverance.

Meditation: "My God, my God, why have you forsaken me?" (Psalm 22:1)

Application: Begin by getting on your knees in a prayer stance. Open the agony of your soul to God and share with him the terrors that you feel. Ask God to show you the way to deliverance. Trust that he will lead you in that direction.

Prayer: O my God, my God, where are you? Have you turned your face from me? Have you abandoned me in this deserted place? Have you left me here to die completely alone? Sometimes, I do feel this way, so alone, as if you are not there and have forsaken me. I feel as if I am insignificant and am nothing at all.

I shudder with the feeling of being alone to suffer in the chaos of these traumatic events. At times I feel so lowly and unimportant, as if nothing can be done for me and no one cares about me. I cry out with a loud voice, "My God, my God, why have you forsaken me?" Deep inside I know these thoughts and feelings are not true, but they are what I feel in times like this.

Send your Holy Spirit, O God, to comfort me and to heal me. Deliver me from this agony that I am experiencing. Be present with me and heal me. In your Holy Name I pray. Amen.

DAY 11

Enemies

Scripture: Psalm 59:1–2

> [1] Deliver me from my enemies, O my God;
> protect me from those who rise up against me;
> [2] deliver me from those who work evil,
> and save me from bloodthirsty men.

Devotional Thoughts: We never enjoy thinking of ourselves as paranoid. Yet, the warrior's behavior after being in the combat zone can mimic paranoia. This paranoid approach to life means that enemies exist everywhere.

In the combat zone, the people who might kill you can be women or children, young or old. No uniforms distinguish the fighting force from the civilian force. Thus, warriors have to be constantly aware of their surroundings, which is called situational awareness.

Innocent backpacks can turn into IEDs (Improvised Explosive Devices). A deserted car on the side of the road can explode as convoys pass. Certain sounds signal the launch of a missile.

Hyper-awareness of all of these threats means avoidance of death. This hyper-awareness becomes a way of life for warriors. The plane ride home across the Atlantic Ocean does not turn off this hyperawareness. Thus, warriors see and sense dangers in places that others do not see or sense dangers.

When warriors attend a school function for their kids, the number of backpacks in the gym can overwhelm combat veterans. The loud stomping on bleachers can mimic the sounds of bombing. A spouse's tone of voice can register as a threat.

The hyper-awareness that is a way of life in the combat zone causes the warrior to interpret enemies everywhere when that warrior returns home. Nightmares, flashbacks, and hyperawareness find enemies throughout the days and the nights for those home from combat.

In this Psalm, David also has actual enemies. Saul has sent men to sit outside of David's house to arrest him—or kill him—if David is home. Every window David looks out has Saul's men lying in wait for him. Anywhere David goes in the kingdom has Saul's men waiting for him. David is unable to tell who will kill him and who will not.

David prays for deliverance from these very real enemies who are surrounding his home and threatening him and his family. David asks God to deliver him and to protect him from his enemies.

Since we know the end of the story, we know that God does deliver David. We know that David becomes King of Israel. In like manner, we can trust that God will deliver us from the enemies that we find inside our minds when we return home from traumatizing events.

The need to be hyper-alert is an excellent combat skill; however, we need to turn down the intensity when we return home. Oftentimes, our spouses are not attacking us when we interpret that they are. The person who just cut us off when we are driving is not really an enemy. The man at the bus stop is just waiting for a bus and is not a predator. The dark is not to be feared, but is just another time of day.

Learning to distinguish who is actually against us and who is for us is a matter of prayer. Dialing down the intensity of hyper-alertness is a necessity so that we can again relate to those around us. Trust that God will help you determine who your enemies are and who is on your side.

Meditation: "Deliver me from my enemies, O my God; protect me from those who rise up against me." (Psalm 59:1)

Application: Make a list of the perceived "enemies" in your life right now. Who and what "feels" like an enemy? Pray that God will give you discernment to understand when you are interpreting people and actions as attacks. Ask him to deliver you from the perceived enemies in your dreams and in your life. Ask him to help you move from the hyper-alert state to one that is more in tune with him.

Prayer: Lord, my Heavenly Father, I come before you opening my heart and soul to you. While I look for peace and joy, I am struggling with locating the normalcy of life. I long to be in a state of peace and calmness; yet, I find myself struggling with employing the skills that I have been taught in preparation for life's confrontations. Are they lying in wait for me just outside of my door? Are they pursuing me as I drive along the highway, just waiting to attack?

Rationally, O God, I know the answer. But my reflexes and internal flight or fight mechanism are ready to engage at a moment's notice. As you did with David, O Lord, protect me from real and perceived enemies. Calm my innermost being. Give me peace while calming the emotions that drive my daily reactions.

May healing be always with me as I drive to work and in my reactions to the family situations that I will encounter in this new day. For your love and peace, I am forever grateful. Now to you, O Lord, be glory, honor, and praise forever. May your holy name be exalted high above the heavens. This is my prayer through Jesus the Christ. Amen.

DAY 12

Crying Out to God

Scripture: Psalm 142:1–7

[1] With my voice I cry out to the LORD;
with my voice I plead for mercy to the LORD.
[2] I pour out my complaint before him;
I tell my trouble before him.
[3] When my spirit faints within me, you know my way!
In the path where I walk they have hidden a trap for me.
[4] Look to the right and see: there is none who takes notice of me;
No refuge remains to me; no one cares for my soul.
[5] I cry to you, O LORD;
I say, "You are my refuge, my portion in the land of the living."
[6] Attend to my cry, for I am brought very low!
Deliver me from my persecutors, for they are too strong for me!
[7] Bring me out of prison, that I may give thanks to your name!
The righteous will surround me, for you will deal bountifully with me.

Devotional Thoughts: When Saul was anointed as the first king of Israel, God's Spirit filled him so that he followed God's way as king. As time passed, Saul chose to veer from the path of God. After Saul disobeyed God several times, God removed his Spirit from Saul.

The Spirit of God moved to David when David was anointed king. The problem was that Saul was still in the physical position as king of Israel. When Saul realized that David was God's anointed one, Saul began the first of several attempts to kill David. In response, David raised an army and fought against Saul.

Psalm 142 was written during this time when David was hiding out from Saul's troops. David and his men lived in caves while Saul's men tried to find them. This Psalm, written from a cave, is David's cry to God during a difficult time.

The words of Psalm 142 give us a language to use when we feel distant from God, when our spirits are weary, and when we need a refuge from life. David begins by crying out to God and by pleading for mercy. We can follow this model, praying to God and asking him for mercy from the spiritual pain that plagues us.

We can also list the challenges that we have. God will hear our prayers that express our spiritual needs, but he also listens to our complaints that life is not the way we thought it would be. David is God's choice for king; yet, he lives in caves and scrounges for food with his men.

In the next verses, David speaks of traps that have been set for him. These traps are literal traps that Saul and his men have placed to capture or kill David and his men. David tells God that his spirit "faints within me." Often, we can feel paranoid as we live our lives. When our lives are upended by trauma, traps can seem to appear everywhere. We can become so overwhelmed that our courage can falter.

Even as David explains to God that he feels alone and that he can find no one to support him, David also states that he knows that God is his refuge. Like David, we often feel that we have no refuge. We feel that no one cares for our soul—our true self. At these times, David teaches us to be confident in God as our refuge. We are never alone because God is with us and he provides bountifully for us.

God refers to David as a "man after God's own heart" because David's life focused on God and his ways. In this Psalm, we understand that David, like us, became discouraged with the circumstances in his life. When this happened, David cried out to God with his frustrations, fears, and alienation. David asked God to pay attention to his needs and to provide refuge for him. We can follow David's example with the confidence that God hears us and will respond.

Meditation: "Bring me out of prison that I may give thanks to your name!" (Psalm 142:7a)

Application: Use the words of this Psalm to voice your own struggles with spiritual pain, frustration, and alienation. Write the verses so that they represent your feelings and pain. Like David, remember that God is with you and will provide a refuge for you.

Use this model in your prayer:

- Begin your prayer by crying out to God. David knows that God will hear him when he cries out to God.
- Follow this by pleading for God's mercy. David turns to God for mercy because he is the one who forgives us when we confess our sins.
- Share your struggles, confusions, and discouragements with God. David openly pours out his complaints and challenges to God. He tells God his struggles.
- Realize and accept that God is your refuge. David explains to God that he feels alone and that he has no support; yet, David claims God as his refuge.

- Ask God to provide a refuge for you to have peace. David asks God to hear him, pay attention to his needs, and provide a refuge for him.

Prayer: O God, I feel as if all I do is cry out to you, listing all of my problems that plague me. I list them one by one and the list is long and cumbersome. What I really wonder about, Lord, is do you really hear me? Do you really care?

I am thankful, Lord, that you hear my cry and allow me to call out to you. You are mighty and compassionate in your care for me. Help me to see where you are working in my life and where you are growing me through these trials. Give me the courage to align with you. It is there where I will find you and be wrapped up in your secure arms.

As I bask in your presence, I take confidence in your Word that encourages me to allow you to be my sanctuary, a place of complete shelter and solitude. Because of your curative touch, I can face tomorrow. Thank you, Lord, and may you always be praised. In the name of Jesus, your Son, I pray. Amen.

DAY 13

Intercession

Scripture: Romans 8:26

> 26 Likewise the Spirit helps us in our weakness. For we do not know what to pray for as we ought, but the Spirit himself intercedes for us with groanings too deep for words.

Devotional Thoughts: From boyhood to college, football was my passion. Weight training, running, and practice strengthened me for the games each Saturday. When I left college for the Marine Corps, running became my passion. When I ran, I could feel the physical power flowing through my body. I liked the feeling, so I continued running.

When I moved from the Marine Corps to the Navy Chaplain Corps, I did not change my running habits. When I was on board a ship, I had to adjust the distance a bit, but I continued the running. I ran on ships, in ice and snow, and in desert heat.

The benefits of distance running for me were the continued physical strength and the power that I felt from it. I could always depend on the feelings of strength that came from running. The strength of my body was something that I came to take for granted.

In like manner, I took my spiritual strength for granted. As a chaplain, I was a bearer of the presence of God to those around me. I understood the need to maintain my spiritual health so I maintained my spiritual disciplines. I had daily devotions and prayer. Often my runs would be part of my prayer time. I would strengthen my physical and spiritual self at the same time. I regularly conducted services and regularly shared the love of God through his Son with military members and their families. My spiritual self was strong, and, like my physical self, I was disciplined in caring for my spiritual self.

When I deployed to Afghanistan and then to Iraq, I maintained my physical and spiritual disciplines. Without my realizing it, I moved into the up-tempo combat pace that changed me in mind, body, and spirit.

When I returned home, I was unaware of how secondary traumatization was weakening my spirit. I knew there was a great distance between God and me, but I did not know how to close that distance. All of my spiritual disciplines were ineffective. After a few years, my spiritual self became very weak.

My physical discipline kept my physical self powerful; however, the daily disciplines of scripture reading and prayer were empty actions for my weakened spirit. I no longer knew how to pray or worship. I had no words to express what I felt in my spirit.

This pattern is common among traumatized people. Many of us have strong relationships with God through his Son, Jesus, before our traumatic experience(s). Then trauma occurs, and we find ourselves unable to hear God or respond to him. Our spirits are plagued with terrors in the night and all of our attempts to use our spiritual disciplines are futile. What worked as spiritual disciplines for us before the trauma, no longer works for us. We are weakened spirits, unable to feel the Spirit of God minister to us.

Romans 8:26 addresses our weakened spirits. When our spirits are traumatized, we often have no words. We only have pain, confusion, and fear. We feel deep shame, guilt, fear, and brokenness. Paul tells us in Romans that the Holy Spirit helps us when our spirits are weak.

Not only does the Holy Spirit help us, but the Holy Spirit also stands before God as our representative. For our deep pain, our traumatized spirit, our moral injury, the Holy Spirit has no words. When we go before God in our weakness, the Holy Spirit intercedes (pleads with God for us) when we are unable to do so. The Holy Spirit groans before God in ways that are deeper than words.

So often when we are traumatized, we find that we can no longer pray. When our protective barriers are too strong, then we block the Holy Spirit from working in our lives. We can trust that the Holy Spirit is working for us. We have to open our spiritual selves to the Holy Spirit in order for the Holy Spirit to represent us before God.

We do not have to have the words. We only need to trust that the Holy Spirit will take our pain, shame, guilt, anger, and brokenness to God in groanings that do not need words.

Meditation: "The Spirit himself intercedes for us with groanings too deep for words." (Romans 8:26)

Application: How strong is your spiritual self? Trauma opens our eyes to the weaknesses in our spiritual lives. Trust that the Holy Spirit will intervene for you. Begin praying the prayer below with confidence in the Holy Spirit's power to respond and God's desire to bring you peace.

Prayer: Father, in the quietness of this moment, be my strength. Cause me to find my new being totally in your existence. Change me, strengthen me, and form me after your likeness. Protect me from the power of all that is contrary to your calling on my life.

Create in me a new foundation of what it means to be totally renewed in body, mind, and spirit. As the groanings of my prayers are lifted to you, may your Spirit intercede and translate them into a sweet-smelling sacrifice of praise to you, O God my Savior. For the newness of life, I am forever grateful.

Now, teach me how to walk in wholeness of life experiencing the growth, the harmony, the recognition of your healing as I experience your active presence in my life. May I groan no more, but instead, sing praises to your name. Hear my prayer, Father in heaven, now and forevermore. Amen

SECTION 2

Endurance Produces Character

"Patience is more than endurance. A saint's life is in the hands of God like a bow and arrow in the hands of an archer. God is aiming at something the saint cannot see, and he stretches and strains, and every now and again the saint says—'I cannot stand anymore.' God does not heed, he goes on stretching till his purpose is in sight, then he lets fly. Trust yourself in God's hands. Maintain your relationship to Jesus Christ by the patience of faith. 'Though he slay me, yet will I trust in him.'"

—*Oswald Chambers*

DAY 14

Walk in Darkness

Scripture: Isaiah 50:10

> [10] Who among you fears the LORD and obeys
> the voice of his servant?
> Let him who walks in darkness and has no light
> trust in the name of the LORD and rely on his God.

Devotional Thoughts: In January 1915, the British explorer ship, *Endurance,* became trapped in Antarctic ice. As the ice grew thicker and thicker around the ship, the crew feared the ship would break apart due to the pressure from the ice. They disembarked and began living on the floating ice that surrounded the ship. Ernest Shackleton, the leader of the expedition, and his men remained in the area on floating ice until April 1916, fifteen months later.

During this time on the ice, the men experienced the darkness of the Antarctic winters. In the southern hemisphere, the winters span March through October and the summers, November through February. Antarctica, considered one of the coldest places on earth, has few items that grow naturally. Those stranded there in the early twentieth century could not farm for food. No one lived at Antarctica and ships did not pass close by. The outlook for their survival was extremely bleak.

The darkness of the Antarctic winters that the *Endurance* crew experienced is a darkness that lasts twenty-four hours a day for about two weeks. Then as the season moves into summer, the sun appears for longer and longer periods each day. After two weeks of complete sunlight, the sunlight fades more and more each day until the complete darkness returns.

This complete darkness, broken up only by brilliant colors appearing in the sky (southern lights), consumes those who live within it. Stars and southern lights were the only natural lighting for these twenty-eight men trapped by the ice. Living on the ice for over a year, the *Endurance* crew battled the elements and existed through two winters. They walked in darkness and had no light.

As April 1916 brought the second winter, the *Endurance* crew used four small boats to travel to an uninhabited island, Elephant Island. From there, Shackleton and a small crew ventured across the turbulent ocean to South Georgia Island from where they launched a rescue attempt for the rest of the crew. In August 1916, Shackleton returned to Elephant Island and successfully brought all twenty-eight members of his crew to safety. The crew of the *Endurance* spent almost two years trapped in the ice of Antarctica.

Despair and darkness often consume our days and nights. We feel stranded on a barren island that continually challenges us to find a way to nurture our relationship with God. At times, darkness fills our minds so completely that we can lose our way. We find no light in our world. We feel abandoned and far from any means of rescue.

Isaiah reminds us that in the midst of darkness when hope seems to be nonexistent, we can trust in God and we can rely on him. Shackleton's crew spent almost two years in a seemingly hopeless situation. They had left England with Shackleton as their protector. They had found themselves in desperate situations. Yet, Shackleton proved to be faithful to the commitment that leaders of expeditions make to those who pursue adventure with them. Shackleton saved his men from death.

God provides for us, planning our rescue, when we are trapped in darkness. What we know of God and our experiences with him from the past provide a basis from which we can rely on his work in our lives. Even if we are stranded with no hope, God will come to us and provide hope for us. We just have to wait with hope as Shackleton and his men in Antarctica did a century ago.

Meditation: "Let him who walks in darkness and has no light trust in the name of the Lord." (Isaiah 50:10b).

Application: Record two times when God was faithful to you. Remember what God has done for you in your life. Even if you find yourself in darkness, pray for God to help you trust him and rely on him.

Prayer: O Father, how faithful you are to me. You are the God of light. Push out the darkness, and fill me with the light of your presence. In days gone by, you have undergirded me with your presence. You have provided for my needs even when I could not see where my sustenance would come from. Steadfastly, you stood with me so that I was never alone.

To know you are there gives me a newfound vigor with which I can face tomorrow. O how resilient I am when you are with me. Be with me forever, Lord. Keep me from falling and plunging to the depths. Lift me up to be the person you have created me to be. In you, I find all my might to face tomorrow. Now may the God of glory be my Protector forever and ever. Amen.

DAY 15

The Edges of Society

Scripture: Luke 8:42b–48

> 42b As Jesus went, the people pressed around him. 43 And
> there was a woman who had had a discharge of blood
> for twelve years, and though she had spent all her living
> on physicians, she could not be healed by anyone. 44 She
> came up behind him and touched the fringe of his gar-
> ment, and immediately her discharge of blood ceased.
> 45 And Jesus said, "Who was it that touched me?" When all
> denied it, Peter said, "Master, the crowds surround you
> and are pressing in on you!" 46 But Jesus said, "Someone
> touched me, for I perceive that power has gone out from
> me." 47 And when the woman saw that she was not hid-
> den, she came trembling, and falling down before him
> declared in the presence of all the people why she had
> touched him, and how she had been immediately healed.
> 48 And he said to her, "Daughter, your faith has made you
> well; go in peace."

Devotional Thoughts: In the Old Testament, the concepts of "clean" and "unclean" are common. These terms describe whether a person is allowed to enter the worship areas. Leviticus 15 discusses the rules for bodily discharges of all kinds and how these discharges make people unclean for worshipping. This scripture also explains how to cleanse the body in order to worship again. People who come in contact with unclean people become unclean as well. They then have to cleanse themselves before they can once again worship.

Over time, Israel developed the practice of isolating people who had long term "unclean" situations. This woman, who had discharged bodily fluids for twelve years, had been isolated for this amount of time as well. She had not been able to worship and she had not been able to participate in social events. She was an outcast from society.

This woman, however, perceived a difference about Jesus as he walked among them. Knowing her place in society, she approached Jesus from behind and touched the edge of his garment. Immediately, she was healed. Jesus responded to her touch and demanded to know who had approached him. Fearful of the punishment that would come to her, the woman acknowledged that she was the one who had touched Jesus. Instead of reprimanding her, Jesus told her that her faith had healed her. Then he told her to go in peace.

According to the law in Leviticus 15, Jesus was technically unclean after the woman touched him. Her emission of bodily fluid made all that she touched unclean. Jesus, however, did not respond to her place in society. Instead, he acknowledged the depth of her faith and pronounced a blessing of peace on her.

The memories that haunt the traumatized and the actions in which they may have participated cause them to feel unclean before God. Often, the Christian community responds as if those whose spirits are wounded by war, rape, or other trauma are "unclean." Thus, the feelings that traumatized people have about themselves are reinforced when they enter churches. Our society can also stereotype people who are traumatized and push them to the edges. Traumatized people can draw the conclusion that God responds to them as the church and society does.

Jesus' response to this woman, however, changed what was "clean" and "unclean" in the worship of his time and of our time. Jesus responded to the faith of the person and not her position in society or her physical condition. He blessed her and gave her peace.

Even though society—Christian or not—may push traumatized persons to the edge, Jesus does not view us that way. He responds to our faith, no matter how small. He embraces us and gives us peace.

Meditation: "Your faith has made you well; go in peace." (Luke 8:48b)

Application: List the areas where you feel that you are an outsider. List actions that you have experienced that make you feel "unclean."

Begin by asking God for his forgiveness as necessary. Then pray that Jesus will touch you and make you *feel* clean. Have faith that he will respond to your request and that he will grant you peace.

Prayer: Lord God, so often I feel unclean and undeserving and therefore not worthy to come into your presence. Still at other times, I cannot even call upon your name out of fear and shame. How I long to be cleansed so that I am free from all my shame. The sins of my youth snap at my heels.

O Lord, how can you forgive a sinner like me? I pray that as I list my sinful actions, you will be gracious to me and forgive each sin, separating them from me as far as the east is from the west. Cleanse my soul, and make me whole and righteous once again in your sight.

Thank you, Father, for forgiving and loving me once again. To you be all glory, honor, and praise. Amen.

DAY 16

Finding a Refuge

Scripture: Psalm 7:1–2

> 1 O Lord my God, in you do I take refuge;
> save me from all my pursuers and deliver me,
> 2 Lest like a lion they tear my soul apart,
> rending it in pieces, with none to deliver.

Devotional Thoughts: In 1913, Theodore Roosevelt visited South America. Fresh from a humiliating defeat for a third term as president, Roosevelt was searching for a new challenge in his life. Roosevelt had been sickly as a child and used that experience to develop a philosophy of life that focused on physical health and well-being. He stressed exercise in all forms as a way to cope with life. His successes in life included leading charges at San Juan Hill with his Rough Riders, being governor of New York, serving almost two terms as U.S. President, establishing many of our national forests, enduring an African safari, and other notable activities. Thus, the loss of a third term as President left Roosevelt humiliated and humbled. He left soon afterwards for a speaking tour in South America.

As he was completing his speaking tour, Teddy Roosevelt answered a challenge to join Colonel Candido Mariano da Silva Rondon, a famous Brazilian explorer, in a journey to map the

River of Doubt. Roosevelt, eager to explore this unknown territory, readily agreed to the challenge. In his life, Roosevelt had found that a physical challenge always helped him as he dealt with tragedies. He knew that a physical challenge always caused the world to "make sense."

The journey began in October 1913 with the team hiking for six weeks to the headwaters of the river. As they began their journey down the river, they became aware that their dugouts—heavy canoes carved out trees—were not the kind of craft needed for this river full of waterfalls and rapids. The heavy dugouts had no flexibility and needed at least two strong men to carry them around the many waterfalls.

As the expedition continued down the river, the explorers' food stores diminished faster than planned and they were plagued by malaria and other fevers. They often had to leave the river and carry their boats downstream to avoid rapids and waterfalls. The insects covered them day and night. After some time on the river, they had only two dugouts since the river had broken apart the other ones. The food supplies were nonexistent and monkey meat was their only sustenance.

All members of the expedition suffered from malaria to some degree. Roosevelt sustained a severe cut to his leg, which became infected. His fever soared and the others fought to keep him alive. In lucid moments, Roosevelt begged them to continue without him. They refused. Weak, starving, and feverish, the men continued the 1,000-mile journey.

Finally, in April 1914, the expedition arrived at a settlement of rubber workers. These families took the former President and his expedition into their homes, providing food and medicines that helped all of them heal. The expedition members found shelter and safety among these people who provided comfort at the end of the harrowing journey.

Roosevelt never recovered his health after this 1,000-mile journey down the River of Doubt. The philosophy of robust health and physical exercise to which Roosevelt had subscribed failed to help him after the harshness of the environment on the river. He continued to have bouts of malaria until his death five years later.

Trauma, like the River of Doubt, happens when our supplies are inadequate, when we are ill-prepared for the dangers we confront, and when our systems are overwhelmed by the challenges before us. Often we begin prepared, but because of the duration or intensity of the trauma, our preparation is not adequate for the challenges we encounter. We find ourselves encountering evil in ways we could not imagine.

When we feel we are pursued and our enemy threatens to tear our souls apart, we can know that God will provide shelter for us. Just as Roosevelt's expedition found comfort at the end of their long journey, we, too, can know that God will provide comfort for us at the end of our spiritual journeys.

David reminds us to take refuge in God when we are pursued by enemies that will tear our souls apart. The darkness of a rainforest river with rapids and dangers contains a refuge for people. God also provides a refuge for us no matter the dark place in which we find ourselves. We are assured of God's protection no matter the dangers we face in this life.

Meditation: "O Lord my God, in you do I take refuge." (Psalm 7:1)

Application: What is the dark journey that you have experienced? Think of this experience and your life since that time. How has God provided refuge for you since that time? Make a list of items that show God's provision for you.

Prayer: Lord, the journey of life can be exhausting and draining as I maneuver through its lengthy and winding paths. The obstacles can be overwhelming, causing discouragement and despair. But you, O Lord, undergird and bolster my ability to go on.

When obstacles crop up, and struggles appear ready to drain my strength and desire to go on, my trust in you never wavers.

Nothing, Almighty God, can cause me to sway as I keep my focus on you. For in you, O Lord, I find a place of care and security.

May your provisions of life continue to give me the sustenance I need to weather the storms and to continue the journey. I rejoice and sing praise to you as I find myself firmly in the refuge of your arms. To the glory of your name, O Most High, I pray. Amen.

DAY 17

God Strengthens Us

Scripture: Isaiah 40:27–31

27 Why do you say, O Jacob,
and speak, O Israel,
"My way is hidden from the LORD,
and my right is disregarded by my God"?
28 Have you not known? Have you not heard?
The LORD is the everlasting God,
the Creator of the ends of the earth.
He does not faint or grow weary;
his understanding is unsearchable.
29 He gives power to the faint,
and to him who has no might he increases strength.
30 Even youths shall faint and be weary,
and young men shall fall exhausted;
31 but they who wait for the LORD shall renew their strength;
they shall mount up with wings like eagles;
they shall run and not be weary;
they shall walk and not faint.

Devotional Thoughts: This passage begins the section of Isaiah that brings a message of hope to the people of Israel during the

Babylonian exile. The focus of this part of Isaiah is on a savior who will deliver the people and on God as the only God.

This scripture is also a powerful passage for those struggling to break free from the bonds of traumatic wounds and of depression that can accompany those wounds. In the midst of trauma and its aftermath, we often feel that God has deserted us. The protective measures that we take to attempt to prevent a reoccurrence of the trauma can also block us from a relationship with God.

This passage begins by challenging the concept that God does not care for us. Why do we claim that our way is hidden from God and that he disregards our needs? Isaiah calls on us—as the Psalmists often do—to remember what we have known about God and to focus on our experiences with God.

If we do this, then we will know that God is the everlasting God who is the Creator of the earth and all that exists. We can depend on him because he is all-powerful. He does not grow tired. But most importantly, his understanding is beyond our comprehension. We know that God understands our pain and our terrors because he created us. Jesus lived through the trauma of the cross. Through his trauma on the cross, we have the hope of eternal life with God.

But in the midst of the aftermath of trauma (PTSD/moral and spiritual injury), we can grow very tired. Keeping up our protections can wear us down. Beginning in verse 29, we find the answer to our weariness. God gives power to the weary. When we have no strength, God will increase our strength. Even young people grow weary and exhausted, but God provides strength for them and for us.

This concept of increasing our strength, however, can be misleading. We are people of the "quick fix" society where a pill or a rapid answer is our goal. The formula for regaining strength in this passage is to wait on the Lord.

When we wait on the Lord, then our focus is on God and not on our own needs. Wait on God and our strength will be renewed. God does not promise a return to our old lives or to the life that we think we deserve. God promises to renew our strength when we wait on him.

In other words, we turn our inner focus to God and submit to his leadership. For those of us who are healing from traumatic wounds, this means to release the protective shell in which we live in so that we can allow God to control our lives. Waiting can be very difficult when we are pursued by terrors and flashbacks. Each time, if we return to an attitude of waiting on God, then slowly, that becomes the habit of our inner being.

God will, in his own time, renew our strength. At this point in these verses, we tend to focus on mounting up with wings like eagles. But the actual verses have three categories of strength—flying, running, and walking.

God does not return us to a previous state, a state of old orientation. After trauma, we know too much about how fragile life is to believe in what had been our "normal" life. Instead, God teaches us his ways: wait and receive strength.

We also have to accept the strength God gives to us. We may only be able to walk without fainting. We need to recognize that God has strengthened us to be able to walk. He provides strength for some to be able to run and not grow weary. He strengthens others to be able to soar with the eagles.

God provides strength to each of us as he chooses. We need to remember what he has done for us in the past. We need to turn to him and wait for God to renew our strength. We need to accept the strength he gives us and be grateful to him for the gift of strength.

Meditation: "But they who wait for the Lord shall renew their strength." (Isaiah 40:31a)

Application: What have you experienced of God's power in the past? Write out a list. Read over this list each day. In prayer, tell God that you are waiting for him to renew your strength. Thank

God for the knowledge you have of him. Ask for strength to wait and then ask for strength to go from one day to the next.

Prayer: Lord, you are holy and full of awesome majesty. Your grandeur is breathtaking to behold. O how magnificent are your courts in the richness of your dwelling place. But on the soil that I walk, your majesty, grandeur, and richness seem to be absent. I long to be found in the safety of your courts.

In the battles of daily life, I fight with despair and loneliness. I long for relief and a sense of hope, O God, that can only be found in you. In you, I have complete confidence. I trust in you who is the only One that can empower me to move through these moments of anguish. It is you, God, who enables me to mount up with wings as eagles, and to run and not be weary.

Now Father, I call upon you to calm me at the core of my being. Calm me, so I can hear your quiet and soothing voice call to me. Strengthen me so that I can walk, run, or soar with eagles. How refreshing it is to rest in the arms of the Almighty. I beseech Thee through this prayer to make it so, Lord Jesus. To your glory I pray. Amen.

DAY 18

Nightmares

Scripture: Psalm 91:1–6

> 1 He who dwells in the shelter of the Most High
> will abide in the shadow of the Almighty.
> 2 I will say to the Lord, "My refuge and my fortress,
> my God, in whom I trust."
> 3 For he will deliver you from the snare of the fowler
> and from the deadly pestilence.
> 4 He will cover you with his pinions,
> and under his wings you will find refuge;
> his faithfulness is a shield and buckler.
> 5 You will not fear the terror of the night,
> nor the arrow that flies by day,
> 6 nor the pestilence that stalks in darkness,
> nor the destruction that wastes at noonday.

Devotional Thoughts: When I was in Iraq, I traveled throughout the Al Anbar Province, supporting chaplains as they supported Marines and sailors. I listened to their stories and I listened to the stories that the Marines and sailors had told the chaplains. As time went by, these stories became my nightmares—my terrors of the night.

I watched—on multiple screens—as one of our helicopters was shot from the sky. A few weeks later, I was on a helicopter that was engaged by ground rocket devices. As we jerked, jenked, turned, and dived to avoid the electronic signal that had locked onto us, we began falling from the sky. Even though the pilots evaded the potential missile, this whole scenario became part of my nightmares.

My nightmares woke me in Iraq. My nightmares woke me for years after I returned home. I feared those terrors of the night as I returned again and again to Iraq. The nightmares were a kind of pestilence—a sickness—that stalked me in the darkness. Deep sleep was hard to find. When I slept, there was destruction that laid waste to wherever I was.

I knew that God was my refuge and fortress. I trusted in him; yet, I lived with the terrors of the night. Arrows flew at me through the days and terror stalked me at night. How could I dwell in the shelter of the Most High when I was surrounded by such destruction and terror? I lived fully in a state of disorientation in my spiritual life.

This Psalm presents God's protection of us. It states that God will deliver us from pestilence and night terrors. He will cover us with his wings so that we can find a refuge.

I longed for this refuge that God could provide. I longed to be free of the terrors of the night. I longed for freedom from the constant wasteland that existed within me. It seemed that I was locked into this place that was so far from God.

But I read the words of this Psalm and I began trying to remember what God had done for me in the past. Slowly, I was able to begin to remember his presence and then I began to feel his presence.

We like band-aids for our spiritual pain. We want quick fixes that take away our struggle. God will provide us with a refuge, but we must wait on him to provide for us. There are times when we can remember what he has done for us in the past, and use that remembrance to comfort us in the present.

God will deliver us when he is ready. He will lead us into a new orientation when we understand his work in our lives. God will provide a refuge for us.

Meditation: "Under his wings you will find refuge." (Psalm 91:4b)

Application: Make a list of the terrors of your dreams. What haunts you through the day? Then make a list of how God has been faithful to you in the past. Read over both lists. Pray for God to deliver you from the terrors. Then thank him for his presence in your life.

Prayer: Father, the dreams that come in the middle of the night are at times horrifying, sleep depriving, and debilitating. They come unannounced, causing fitful nights. In the terror of the night, I call on you, O God, to come and deliver me from the pestilence that stalks me by night.

How faithful you are always to be here, listening to my prayerful cries for your presence. Father, like you have done each night, come and be my refuge and fortress. I feel safe and secure when I know your presence is with me. I sleep more soundly and find newness of life as your hand rests upon me.

For your faithful care, O God, I give you thanks. I am forever grateful and trust in you with my whole life and being. I have hope for deliverance and healing from the despair and fear that used to rule my life. In the light of your Son, I praise you all day long for you are my God forever and ever. In your holy name, I pray. Amen.

DAY 19

Overwhelming Grief

Scripture: Psalm 73:26

> 26 My flesh and my heart may fail, but God is the strength of my heart and my portion forever.

Devotional Thoughts: Abraham Lincoln, the sixteenth President of the United States, had arguably the most traumatic presidency on record. Within a month after his election, South Carolina seceded from the U.S. Several other states followed over the next months. Between Lincoln's November 1860 election and his March 1861 inauguration, the United States had split into two countries.

The month following Lincoln's inauguration marked the beginning of the Civil War. The country that elected Lincoln had split into two countries and had begun to fight each other. The first few years of the Civil War went poorly for the Union forces, causing Lincoln to change commanding generals often.

In late 1861, General George B. McClellan commanded the Army of the Potomac. Lincoln and McClellan often disagreed about the policies affecting the war. McClellan refused to use his forces to their highest capability, causing the Union troops to suffer many defeats and resulting in the deaths of many soldiers. Lincoln routinely pressed McClellan to attack and defeat the Confederate troops. Refusing to follow Lincoln's guidance,

McClellan continued to be defeated and the loss of life on both sides continued to compound.

Early in 1862, Lincoln, his wife, and his two younger sons, Willie and Tad, were living in the White House. Their oldest son, Robert, was at Harvard. Their second son, Edward, had died years before at the age of three. With both younger boys lying ill, Lincoln continued to run the country and the war. Checking in often on the boys (who were in separate rooms), President Lincoln would return to meetings and to the decision-making required of a President during war time.

Willie died of this illness at age eleven. The President and his family were devastated. Mary Todd Lincoln sank into a severe depression and refused to attend the funeral. Tad, still sick but recovering, was left without his closest friend and playmate when his brother died.

Losing battle after battle, losing his son, and dealing with his wife's declining mental health, Abraham Lincoln had little time to grieve with the families losing their sons and fathers, with his country that was torn apart, or with his family that had just lost their sweetest member.

Lincoln's prayer could be that of Psalm 73: 26. His flesh and his heart were failing as he grieved for this precious son and for the sons of those on both sides of the war. Yet, Lincoln continued to lean on God for wisdom and strength. As mother after mother, wife after wife, sister after sister paraded through the White House to meet with the President to beg for the lives of their sons, husbands, and brothers, Lincoln met with them and did what he could to discover the fate of those lost Union soldiers. The weight of a nation—broken in two—was on Lincoln's shoulders.

Lincoln's grief for the tremendous loss of a nation and those fighting for and against it as well as for the loss of his son continued throughout the war. Lincoln's words after the Battle of Gettysburg encapsulate the grief that he felt as he mourned for these losses. Abraham Lincoln said in his "Gettysburg Address":

> But, in a larger sense, we can not [sic] dedicate—we can not consecrate—we can not hallow—this ground. The brave men, living and dead, who struggled here, have consecrated it, far above our poor power to add or detract. The world will little note, nor long remember what we say here, but it can never forget what they did here. It is for us the living, rather, to be dedicated here to the unfinished work which they who fought here have thus far so nobly advanced. (Lincoln, 2002)

In our culture today, we have professionals trained to handle traumatic incidents and who know how to react when the times are tough. These professionals include law enforcement, fire fighters, and military, who are trained to run toward a traumatic happening while others run away. Chaplains, health care professionals, and ministers are trained to counsel people in crisis. We have specialty care people who focus on trauma care and recovery.

The time comes, however, when these professionals, like Lincoln, can become overwhelmed with the weight of the losses that they are facing. They feel the pain of those who lose loved ones, who wonder what they could have done differently, and of their own losses. They feel that their flesh and hearts may fail.

When we become overwhelmed with grief, our spirits can recoil from the experiences because of such intense trauma. We feel the weight of all that has transpired and collected within our minds and spirits. Like Lincoln, we have to continue with our daily routines.

In these times, remember that God is your strength. Even if you find that you can no longer move through your day, remember that you are part of the ongoing work of those who have given their lives before you. God gives us strength to move on, day-by-day, or moment by moment. Trust him.

Meditation: "God is the strength of my heart." (Psalm 73:26b)

Application: Do you feel that you are carrying a great burden of grief and loss? Do you feel that your heart and spirit cannot continue much longer? Make a list of the people for whom you are grieving and the losses that you feel. Tell God that you are unable to continue and ask him to renew your strength. He will come to you and give you the strength you need to continue.

Prayer: God in heaven, to you I turn as my strength seems to waver. Sometimes the grief I bear overwhelms me and I can barely move, think, or participate in my daily responsibilities. The weight of the day's happenings coupled with the quiet battles within the recesses of my mind at night are tearing me apart.

Where are you in the midst of this grief, shame, and despair? Make yourself known to me, O Lord, and deliver me from the snare of my own inner wounds. Strengthen me by day and give me peace and tranquility by night. Help me forever to feel the safety of your presence as I move through the aftermath of a distressed heart. Healing and hope can only come from you. Lord, be my portion forever. In the name above all names, Jesus Christ. Amen.

DAY 20

Adequate Fortresses

Scripture: Psalm 31:1–4

> [1] In you, O LORD, do I take refuge; let me never be put to
> shame; in your righteousness deliver me!
> [2] Incline your ear to me; rescue me speedily!
> Be a rock of refuge for me, a strong fortress to save me!
> [3] For you are my rock and my fortress;
> and for your name's sake you lead me and guide me;
> [4] You take me out of the net they have hidden for me,
> for you are my refuge.

Devotional Thoughts: In the 1920s, farmers and ranchers settled the prairie lands of the United States. Farmers plowed up the indigenous grasses that held the fine soils in place so that they could plant wheat and other crops. These high demand crops drank the nutrients out of the soil, causing the crops to dry up.

Ranchers overgrazed these areas as well. The sheep and cattle consumed the grasses of the plains and panhandles in the central United States. These areas then suffered a severe drought. With no native grasses to find waters deep in the barren ground, the areas became the host of severe dust storms.

The winds in these areas, which were named "The Dust Bowl," collected the topsoil and loose dirt to form massive dust storms. These dust storms encompassed large areas, with some even continuing to the East Coast.

People in the plains areas boarded their windows, covered each crevice in their houses, and lived with their faces covered. Animals choked to death on the dust. Young children and older adults suffered from a lung illness caused by inhaling dust.

As dust storm after dust storm rolled through the plains, people of all ages began to contract these lung illnesses. They could not find a refuge from the storm. Dust was in their food, their water, their air, and their homes. As the monstrous clouds of dust poured over the plains, people found no refuge. They had no fortress to protect them from the dust-laden winds.

David's Psalm discusses how God had removed David from the net that had been cast for him. David describes God as a refuge, a fortress, and a rock. Confidant in God's leadership, David reminds us that God is our protection and that he will save us from shame and terror.

Trauma often enters our lives as the dust did for those in the 1930s Dust Bowl. When the traumatic memories rise up as giant dust clouds, we stand paralyzed as the massive cloud of memories moves toward us. Even if we try to protect ourselves, we are unable to keep the memories from rolling over us. We can try to plug each hole, but the prevalence of the traumatic incident fills our minds, spirits, and lives. There is no way to truly protect ourselves from these memories.

This Psalm, however, reminds us that when we are unable to protect ourselves from traumatic memories, that God is there to be a refuge for us. He is a strong fortress who will protect us when the memories wash over us. He is our rock against the storm.

The difficult part, however, is that we want the memories to stop. We want to be free from these memories and the effects they have on our lives. When God does not free us from them, then we claim that he does not care.

God is a strong fortress, providing protection for us when we are in storms that bring darkness and fear. He is with us as we experience these storms in life, in the same way that he was with David. Just as the methods of the Dust Bowl residents were inadequate to protect them from the dust storms, the fortresses that we establish within ourselves to protect us from storms are also inadequate.

Our true fortress, refuge, and protection is found in God's presence. God is an adequate fortress for the darkness in our lives.

Meditation: "Be a rock of refuge for me, a strong fortress to save me!" (Psalm 31:2b)

Application: Consider what ways you protect yourself from the dark storms in your spirit. What are the protections you use to ward off traumatic memories? Are those protective measures preventing you from experiencing God as a fortress and protector?

Pray that God will show you the inadequate protections in your life. Ask God to be your fortress.

Prayer: Gracious God, I call on you to be my refuge, a place where I can find shelter. When the dark clouds come upon me and cover my being, I feel as if I am alone and you have forgotten me. The difficulties of life are the clouds that roll in and cause great wounds. The memories of these traumatic events are seared into my mind forever. At times, those memories become debilitating. In these times of despair, it is hard to move, think, and live life.

Come to me, O God, and let me know your presence. Touch me with your hand of care that delivers and protects in just one touch. You are the reason I can face tomorrow. Undergird me and cause me to have the hope that can only be found in you. May a new peace and assurance of your love be with me for the rest of my days. In your great name I pray, O Lord. Amen.

DAY 21

Isolation

Scripture: Psalm 55:4–8

> 4 My heart is in anguish within me;
> the terrors of death have fallen upon me.
> 5 Fear and trembling come upon me,
> and horror overwhelms me.
> 6 And I say, "Oh, that I had wings like a dove!
> I would fly away and be at rest;
> 7 yes, I would wander far away;
> I would lodge in the wilderness; Selah
> 8 I would hurry to find a shelter
> from the raging wind and tempest."

Devotional Thoughts: George Mallory, a British mountaineer, was a member of the exclusive Alpine Club that was only for the most elite climbers. Living in the late 1800s and early 1900s, Mallory was part of British expeditions exploring areas of the world where few Westerners had gone.

Mallory impressed the Alpine Club members with his climbing skills in the Alps. He was chosen to make one of the first trips by Europeans to Mount Everest. During this early trip, Mallory and his climbing team began by first locating which mountain was Everest. They then attempted to climb parts of the mountain, but harsh winds drove them back.

Instead of another climbing attempt, the team mapped the areas around the base of Everest. Mallory and some other climbers planned a possible route on the northern face of Everest for the next climbing season. Mallory's ability to plan new trails in difficult settings was well known throughout the climbing world.

The climbers returned to England with their information and planned for a second attempt at the summit of Everest. When Mallory returned with a new team the next year, he was again disappointed with the results. Their attempt to climb Everest was thwarted by high winds and snows. They also discovered that they needed oxygen when they reached a certain height. The group returned to England without reaching the summit.

Mallory's third attempt to climb Everest was in 1924. By that time, oxygen was available in canisters that the climbers brought with them. The men climbed high onto Everest's face. Fog had settled on the top of the mountain and several of the men decided to stop. Mallory and another hiker, Andrew Irvine, continued on, aiming for the top of Everest.

Later in the day, there was a break in the fog and the two men were spotted by one of the men lower on the mountain. That was the last time Mallory and Irvine were seen alive. Snow began falling after the fog closed in around the two climbers.

In 1999, an expedition launched to attempt to locate Mallory's body and possibly Irvine's in response to a Chinese climber finding a British body the year before. When the expedition found Mallory's body, they noted several injuries to his body. Mallory had broken bones in his leg, indicating he had taken a serious fall. He also had a deep puncture wound on his forehead, which could potentially have come from his ice axe as he slid down the mountain.

Whether Mallory and Irvine reached the summit remains a question that cannot be answered. If they did reach the summit, then they accomplished it thirty years before the next Westerner was able to do so.

Mallory's last attempt to climb Everest ended in a tragic accident. As he lay alone on the side of the mountain, the terrors of death must have surrounded him. Fear and horror must have overwhelmed him as he realized that his leg would not allow him to walk down the mountain.

In the midst of this trauma, Mallory would have remembered his wife and three children. The desire of the Psalmist to fly away like a dove and be at rest could have been Mallory's wish as well. Finding shelter from the raging wind and snow was impossible for Mallory as he breathed his last. Mallory died alone on the side of Mount Everest.

We, like Mallory, can find ourselves at the end of a long fall, isolated, wounded, and unable to move. The injuries that trauma causes to our spirits can make moving forward seem impossible. We lie alone, waiting for death to come to us.

God has provided a way for us to move from this place of death and horrors, even if we feel frozen in misery. God provides a shelter for us from the raging wind and the tempest. He is our shelter in our time of need.

Most of all, God is with us. We are not alone. Trust him to help you find your way off the mountain and into his warmth and shelter.

Meditation: "Oh, that I had wings like a dove! I would fly away and be at rest." (Psalm 55:6)

Application: Begin by making a list of how God is in your life at this time. List the items and ask God to help you become aware of his presence in your life. Ask God to deliver you from the horrors and the trauma that you experience. Ask him to help you find your way forward. Believe that he will provide a shelter for you. Know that he is with you and you are not alone.

Prayer: To be on the mountaintop, Lord, is thrilling. It feels so safe and far away from anything that can harm me. It is almost like I can reach out and touch heaven and walk right into your dwelling place.

Then reality hits and we must come down the mountain to live life in the valley. It is there we need your ever-loving care and protection. Since life takes place off the mountaintops, we ask that you provide for us in all of our needs. I pray for your Spirit to calm the winds that cause us to dread what lies ahead of us in this life. Be our shelter from the tempest of the raging winds that blow in this life. Bless us, we pray, in Jesus' name. Amen.

"We are not made for the mountains, for sunrises, or for the other beautiful attractions in life—those are simply intended to be moments of inspiration. We are made for the valley and the ordinary things of life and that is where we have to prove our stamina and strength."

—*Oswald Chambers*

DAY 22

God at Work

Scripture: Philippians 2:12–13

> [12] Therefore, my beloved, as you have always obeyed, so now, not only as in my presence but much more in my absence, work out your own salvation with fear and trembling, [13] for it is God who works in you, both to will and to work for his good pleasure.

Devotional Thoughts: Dietrich Bonheoffer, a German theologian, understood the meaning of obedience to God, no matter the cost. Living in Germany as Hitler rose to power, Bonheoffer spoke out against the policies of the Nazi regime. He assisted Jews in escaping from Germany and continually fought the racism directed at Jews in Germany.

At one point, Bonheoffer left Germany for the United States. He spent time lecturing in the U.S., but soon grew restless. He felt God's leadership to return to Germany and fight against the evil there.

Upon his return, Bonheoffer continued his work assisting Jews escaping from Hitler's grip. He also was privy to plots to assassinate Hitler. The Nazis arrested him, jailing him for two years.

In Bonheoffer's example, we witness a pastor/theologian defy civil authorities to rescue people. More than that, however, we see a pastor/theologian participate in the plans for the murder of a head of state. Why would a Christian participate in these behaviors?

Many explanations exist for Bonheoffer's actions. At this point in history, we applaud his rescuing of the Jews because we have the record of how many Jews were killed under Hitler. Participation in an assassination plot is difficult to explain.

These actions are some of those that fall under the words of Paul, "work out your own salvation with fear and trembling." Jesus provided salvation for us through his death. This verse means "sanctification" more than salvation. We should work out our actions with fear and trembling, because God works within us.

Our authentic self, the self that is as authentic as Jesus was, responds to the leadership of the Holy Spirit (Grant, 1996, p. 89). We do not always have a rubber stamp that says "yes" or "no" to our actions. Thus, we are left to trust that God is working within us.

When we suffer, we can know that God is at work in us "both to will and to work for his good pleasure." God can take whatever is happening to us and use it for his good pleasure. For Bonheoffer, this concept means that he learned to judge people differently. He states, "We must learn to regard people less in the light of what they do or omit to do, and more in the light of what they suffer" (1991, p. 262).

The aftereffects of our trauma allow God to work within our lives, drawing us closer to him. The lessons of our trauma include learning to see others through the light provided by their wounds. We learn to judge less and to view our fellow travelers with more compassion.

Bonheoffer was hanged a month before the Allies reached the prison he was in. Seemingly a pointless death, God has worked powerfully through Bonheoffer's writings since that time. These writings have shaped Christian theology throughout the twentieth and into the twenty-first centuries.

Meditation: "For it is God who works in you." (Philippians 2:13)

Application: How do you want people to view you? List ways that you know that God is at work within you. How have the aftereffects of your trauma changed your view of others? Practice looking at others through their woundedness.

Prayer: My woundedness, Lord, haunts me and causes great anguish in many areas of my life. I trust that you, O God, are fast at work within me, initiating adjustments and renovating the innermost places of my life. With fear and trembling, my life goes on. I am obedient to your Word as I work out my salvation with a sense of awe. May my relationship with you shape me to be the person you have designed me to be.

Now, my Father, be my shield and strength as I stand against the raging thoughts and moods that sometimes seem to flow so freely. It is, without a doubt, you that I trust and depend upon. For you are my motivation. Perseverance enables me to step into tomorrow. Continue to give me the faith, love, and drive to be faithful to your calling on my life. For your blessings and healing, I am grateful and am forever praising your Holy name. *Gloria in excelsis Deo.* Amen.

DAY 23

Pain in Our Spirits

Scripture: Mark 14:33–37

> [33] And [Jesus] took with him Peter and James and John,
> and began to be greatly distressed and troubled. [34] And he
> said to them, "My soul is very sorrowful, even to death.
> Remain here and watch." [35] And going a little farther, he
> fell on the ground and prayed that, if it were possible,
> the hour might pass from him. [36] And he said, "Abba,
> Father, all things are possible for you. Remove this cup
> from me. Yet not what I will, but what you will." [37] And
> he came and found them sleeping.

Devotional Thoughts: On the night before he died, Jesus took three of his closest friends, Peter, James, and John, to the Garden of Gethsemane. Knowing what was before him, Jesus went to a private place to pray. He moved away from his friends, asking them to keep watch.

These three men had been with Jesus for three years. They had seen his miracles, sat for his teachings, and aided him with his work. They were close and had been through much; yet, these three failed to understand the intensity of Jesus' emotions at this time. Jesus even told them that he was "very sorrowful, even to death." After sharing the depth of his sorrow, Jesus moved away from the three men to pray. His expectation was that they would be keeping watch for him.

With this expectation that his friends "had his back," Jesus went to pray. The intensity of his prayer as he faced an agonizing death the next day is evident in the scripture. Asking God to bring about the salvation of humankind another way, Jesus asked God to "let this cup pass from me."

Jesus wrestled with the traumatic experiences that awaited him the next day. His death, necessary for our salvation, was not an experience that Jesus rushed to embrace. The importance of his prayer, however, is in his obedience of "not my will, but your will be done." Jesus shares the agony of his soul with God. Jesus states his own preference for events. He ends with submission to God's will.

In the midst of this spiritual agony, Jesus counts on his friends to be keeping watch; yet, when he returns, Jesus finds all three of them asleep. The disciples do not understand the true agony of Jesus' soul. They cannot understand the spiritual pain that he is suffering. Jesus' friends do not understand his spiritual agony until they have the benefit of hindsight.

This story provides several insights into Jesus' life. He knows what spiritual agony is, he knows that God is a refuge in those times, and he experienced friends who did not understand his spiritual pain. His friends failed to understand because they had no reference point. They truly did not understand that Jesus would die in agony the next day and, thus, they were not supportive of Jesus' needs.

When we struggle with deep spiritual pain, our family and friends may mean well, but they "fall asleep" when we need them to stand watch for us. We need understanding, but those who are close to us may lack the ability to understand the depth of our spiritual pain that trauma caused.

This story teaches us that God is able to listen to our cries of pain. As with Jesus, God may not change the circumstances that we are in, but he listens to us and he cares about our agony.

Measuring how deeply people around us care for us by whether or not they understand our spiritual pain is not the measurement that we should use. Jesus' disciples stayed with him during this time of spiritual unrest; yet, they fell asleep. His friends were unable to provide the support that Jesus needed, but God was able to provide it for him.

Trust God to provide for you. Trust him to understand the agony in your spirit. He cares for you and he will bring you to a place of peace.

Meditation: "Yet not what I will, but what you will." (Mark 14:36b)

Application: Think of your closest relationships. Are these people attempting to provide support for you, but, like the disciples, are "falling asleep" when you need them to have your back? Consider the expectations that you have for these people close to you. Begin taking your spiritual agony to God. Share the spiritual pain with him. Allow the people who are close to you to love you, but consider the possibility of changing your expectations of them.

Prayer: Come to me, O Lord, and be with me. At times, I feel as if I am the only one here who understands my spiritual pain. I fear that you are not there; however, you have always been faithful and steadfast in your love, care, and presence in my life. Help me to remember that you are there even when others seem to be sleeping and not engaged.

My spirit is thirsty and longs for the refreshing touch that only you can provide. Be with me in all I do in this day. Give me the ability to cope and to go on. I trust in you, O God, even when my faith wavers, I look to heaven with confidence that you are with me.

In the healing you provide to me, gracious Father, I find a newness of life that causes me to praise you all the day long. To you be glory and honor and praise now and forevermore, O most high and Holy God, Lord of my life. Amen.

DAY 24

Shame

Scripture: John 21:15–17

> 15 When they had finished breakfast, Jesus said to Simon
> Peter, "Simon, son of John, do you love me more than
> these?" Peter said to him, "Yes, Lord; you know that I
> love you." Jesus said to Peter, "Feed my lambs." 16 Jesus
> said to Peter a second time, "Simon, son of John, do
> you love me?" Peter said to him, "Yes, Lord; you know
> that I love you." Jesus said to Peter, "Tend my sheep."
> 17 Jesus said to Peter the third time, "Simon, son of John,
> do you love me?" Peter was grieved because Jesus said to
> him the third time, "Do you love me?" and Peter said to
> him, "Lord, you know everything; you know that I love
> you." Jesus said to him, "Feed my sheep."

Devotional Thoughts: Simon Peter was one of the first disciples that Jesus called. Jesus came to Peter one day while Peter was at work. A fisherman by trade, Peter immediately dropped his nets and followed Jesus. Peter responded with a deep faith when he dropped his livelihood—the one that fed his family—and followed Jesus.

Later when Jesus asked, "Who do people say that I am?" Peter immediately answered with a declaration of Jesus' role in the Godhead. "You are the Christ, the Son of the living God" (Matthew 16:16). Peter recognizes Jesus' place in creation.

Jesus responds to Peter by saying the only way Peter could know this information was if God had told him. Jesus then tells Peter, "[18] And I tell you, you are Peter, and on this rock I will build my church, and the gates of hell shall not prevail against it. [19] I will give you the keys of the kingdom of heaven, and whatever you bind on earth shall be bound in heaven, and whatever you loose on earth shall be loosed in heaven" (Matthew 16:18–19).

Thus, because of Peter's declaration, Jesus says that Peter is the rock on which he will build his church. Peter will also receive the keys to heaven with great power accompanying that reward. Jesus sets Peter apart from all of his other disciples because of Peter's faithfulness.

But times change for Peter. When Jesus is arrested, Peter does little to help him. Jesus had predicted that Peter would deny him three times. Peter was indignant and stated that he would never deny Jesus. After all, Peter had been set apart as a leader by Jesus.

Yet when Jesus is arrested, Peter hangs back. Then Peter creeps into the courtyard of the place where Jesus is held. Three times someone asks if Peter knows Jesus, and three times, Peter denies knowing Jesus. We do not know Peter's motives—possibly he was working up a plan to rescue Jesus. We only know Peter's actions. He denied that he knew Jesus.

Filled with shame, Peter leaves the area. At the lowest point of his life, Peter returns to what he had known—fishing. Peter goes from the rock on which Jesus would build his church to the coward who does not support his Lord. Peter, the keeper of the keys to heaven, is a man who has no backbone. Ashamed and afraid, Peter is not the man he thought himself to be.

After his death, Jesus comes to Peter while Peter is fishing. When Peter comes to shore with a boatload of fish, Jesus and Peter eat together. Jesus then poses three questions to Peter.

Three times, Jesus asks Peter, "Do you love me?" and three times, Peter answers, "Yes." By the third time, Peter is agitated. Jesus knew beforehand that Peter would deny him. Peter, even with foreknowledge, had still denied Jesus. The shame that filled Peter must have made him very uncomfortable by the time Jesus asked him the third question.

Each time that Peter answered, "Yes," Jesus responded with a command to take care of Jesus' people. Peter denied Jesus three times and then Peter received three commands from Jesus to take care of his sheep. In this, Jesus changes Peter's focus from the shame of Peter's past actions to the task that waited for Peter.

Peter's choice to return to his old ways—fishing—was overridden by the commitment that Peter had made to Jesus and that Jesus had made to Peter. Ashamed of his actions and his failure to perform, Peter was lost in that world. Jesus showed Peter that he had a mission to fulfill on earth. He pointed Peter to the future.

We live with the shame of our participation in the traumatic events that occurred in our lives. We are filled with shame for a multitude of reasons—for failure to live up to what we thought we were, for what we feel is cowardice, and for our own participation in events. Just like Peter, Jesus comes to us to point us to the future, to what he can do with us, instead of focusing on our past shame.

Peter took the challenge Jesus issued that day and became one of the strongest leaders in the early church. We can use Peter's example to embrace the forgiveness that God offers us through his Son, Jesus. God will forgive whatever has caused us shame—he forgives whatever we have done if we ask.

Embrace the forgiveness and look forward to the tasks that God will give you for the future. Past actions do not prevent us from being used by God in this world.

Meditation: "Lord, you know everything; you know that I love you." (John 21:17b)

Application: List the sources of shame that you feel. Pray about the list and ask God to let you see these items through his eyes. One by one begin to leave each item behind. Confess your role and accept God's forgiveness. Repeat this prayer often, knowing that God forgives you. Then ask God for the role he has in store for you.

Prayer: O Lord Jesus, you are the Christ, the Son of the living God. To you I lift my arms in honor, praise, and exultation, singing glory to your name in the highest heavens. For you, O Lord, are worthy to be praised, again and again and again.

Lord, I remember the times that I failed you and am ashamed of the sin that still makes its home in my mind. Even though I read in your word that you forgive my sins and throw them into the deepest part of the sea, I still condemn myself for the transgressions and shortcomings of past endeavors.

I remember how you came to Peter by the shores of Galilee and asked him if he loved you three times. Help me to accept fully your love and forgiveness. Heal me and make me whole once again. Then, Lord Jesus, as you did with Peter, empower me to go and feed your sheep once again. In your loving name I pray, Amen.

DAY 25

Facing Spiritual Pain

Scripture: John 12:27–28a

> 27 "Now is my soul troubled. And what shall I say? 'Father,
> save me from this hour'? But for this purpose I have
> come to this hour. 28 Father, glorify your name."

Devotional Thoughts: Escape from pain is the goal of most Americans. We use pain medications, physical therapy, massage therapy, and doctor visits to offset physical pain. Medications, counseling, and exercise often offset mental and emotional pain. We are a pain-adverse culture.

We do have one segment of our society that embraces some kinds of pain. The motto, "No pain, no gain" is part of this segment. Their line of thought is that physical strength comes from physical pain. That pain, however, comes from exercise and pushing to the next level.

In the final week of his life, Jesus makes a triumphal entry into Jerusalem. We celebrate Palm Sunday the week before Easter to commemorate this event. Jesus knew that his life on earth was almost at an end. He spoke of this fact to the crowd.

In John 12, Jesus confesses that his soul is troubled. He is unsettled spiritually and emotionally. Jesus understands what lies ahead for him—intense physical, emotional, and spiritual pain.

Jesus then asks these rhetorical questions: "And what shall I say? 'Father save me from this hour?'" Jesus asks those people around him if he should ask to be saved from the horror of what was before him. That answer is often our answer when we find ourselves in trauma. We ask God to prevent the event or to free us from it.

The power in Jesus' next statement is immense: "But for this purpose I have come to this hour." Jesus recognizes his mission on earth—to be the Savior to all. A blood sacrifice is required—Jesus' blood is required—for the remission of humankind's sins.

Jesus recognizes that avoiding pain means not fulfilling the mission God gave Jesus when he came to earth. Jesus' purpose was to be the sacrifice for the sins of all humans. So the simple statement that he came for this reason and that Jesus has to fulfill his purpose is a powerful lesson for us.

The cross was the final goal for Jesus. Humiliation from crowds, desertion by his friends, intense physical pain, brutal emotional pain, and terrifying spiritual pain awaited Jesus; yet, he did not turn away. He embraced the mission God gave him—no matter the costs in pain and suffering. "For this purpose, I have come to earth."

We rarely think of intense spiritual, emotional, or physical pain as a way to fulfill God's purpose for us. These verses are difficult because of the call to us to respond to God in any circumstance. Pain can be a way to a deeper relationship with God.

Pain for the sake of pain, however, is not the way of Jesus. The final words in this quote read, "Father, glorify your name." Jesus accepts what is before him and asks that through Jesus' actions, God might be glorified.

Trauma provides us with deep spiritual, physical, and emotional pain. Escaping the pain is not always the goal of our Heavenly Father. We, like Jesus, can glorify God if we surrender to his will for our lives. We can find our purpose for being on this earth through the leading of the Holy Spirit. Pain can be the way that we move into a deeper relationship with God. Bringing glory to God should be our focus as we move through our day.

Meditation: "For this purpose I have come to this hour." (John 12:27b)

Application: On a sheet of paper, draw three columns. At the top of one, write "Physical Pain," then "Emotional Pain," and then "Spiritual Pain." In each column, list the pain that you have that fits in each category. Prayerfully consider your responses to each kind of pain. Do you try to avoid the pain? Or do you, like Jesus, ask that God will be glorified through your trials and difficulties? Ask God for guidance as you sort out the pain and your relationship to it.

Prayer: Heavenly Father, sometimes in life I feel all alone, as if there is no one else standing on this earth except me. I know that I am only one of billions of people living on this earth. Yet, I feel alone as I walk through the circumstances of life. I think I almost understand what Jesus must have felt like in the clutches of the Romans before his crucifixion. His followers left him alone in the midst of false accusations. How he must have agonized over the sense of being alone.

While the flesh is weak at times, I am grateful that you are strong and ever vigilant against the one prowling around to devour me. Your presence, Lord, provides comfort and a sense of peace amid fear, pain, and confusion concerning what is next in my life.

Be my confidence as I go forward today. Glorify your name through me in each hour of this day. I give you all that I am. Use me completely for your glory. In the name of the Most High God and the Lord Jesus Christ, I pray. Amen.

DAY 26

God Remembers Us

Scripture: Genesis 8:8–12

> [8] Then [Noah] sent forth a dove from him, to see if
> the waters had subsided from the face of the ground.
> [9] But the dove found no place to set her foot, and she
> returned to him to the ark, for the waters were still on
> the face of the whole earth. So he put out his hand and
> took her and brought her into the ark with him. [10] He
> waited another seven days, and again he sent forth the
> dove out of the ark. [11] And the dove came back to him
> in the evening, and behold, in her mouth was a freshly
> plucked olive leaf. So Noah knew that the waters had
> subsided from the earth. [12] Then he waited another
> seven days and sent forth the dove, and she did not
> return to him anymore.

Devotional Thoughts: Noah was a righteous man who followed God's way while evil and corruption ruled the rest of the earth. God decided to destroy the earth and, effectively, start over. God instructed Noah to build an ark of certain specifications which could carry Noah, his wife, his sons and their wives, and two of each living thing—birds, animals, reptiles, etc.—on earth.

Noah obeyed God, building the ark, gathering what God told him to get, and entering the ark with his family. At that point, the rains began.

The waters poured out from the earth and rain fell until every living creature on earth was drowned. The rain continued for forty days and forty nights. Noah and his family remained in the ark.

In Hebrew, numbers can have significance. The number "forty" is the number for trials and testing. Thus, when we read "forty days" or "forty years" in Biblical accounts, we can understand that God is providing that person(s) with a time of trial and testing.

Noah and his family remained faithful to God throughout the time of the rains. They remained on the ark for 150 days after the rain stopped. Scripture states that God remembered Noah and his family. When God is ready to act after a time of trial and testing, scripture will say that God "remembered the people." In this case, God remembered Noah (Genesis 8) and the waters began to subside. Noah and his family waited several more months before the waters had subsided enough to consider leaving the ark.

When the ark came to rest on a mountain, Noah sent out a raven with no results. Then Noah sent a dove to see if the ground was dry. The dove returned with no evidence of dry ground. Noah sent the dove out a week later and the dove returned with an olive branch in its mouth.

At that point, Noah knew that they could leave their protective ark and begin a new life on the earth. Because of his faithfulness, God established a covenant with Noah in which God pledged never again to destroy the earth by water. The rainbow in the sky is the sign of this covenant (Genesis 9).

People who are traumatized find themselves constructing arks of protection in order to survive in the world around them. These arks protect them from threats and dangers that lurk in strangers, in new places, through doorways, or around corners.

Traumatized people can become locked into their self-protective casings in order to avoid further pain.

The struggle of people with PTSD/moral and spiritual injury is to come out of that protective casing. The protection actually serves to block access to God as well as to protect these people. God calls us to leave our protective shells and to make ourselves vulnerable to his Spirit.

The example of Noah—who entered the ark to protect his family from overwhelming flooding—teaches that protection is necessary at times. We can live in a protective state when necessary, but we also must realize that the time comes when we must begin our journey out of this protection.

Imagine Noah and his family deciding to remain on the ark in case the flooding began again. We have heard this story so often as children that we take it for granted that all of Noah's family readily left the ark. They had just witnessed flooding that covered the entire earth, including the tallest mountains. What if the floods came again? Maybe they should stay near the ark just in case a flood comes again.

Instead, Noah, through a series of attempts, finally received the security he needed to open the doors. The dove returned with an olive branch that it had gotten from a plant that grows in the dirt—dry ground.

Noah and his family left their protective cover. They left the protection of the ark and moved directly into God's protection. The result was that God rewarded Noah's faithfulness and obedience with a promise not to destroy the earth again by water.

God calls to us to step out of the inner shell that we construct to protect ourselves from traumatic happenings. He calls to us to trust his protection of us. He desires that we learn to understand his healing and trust him to protect our spirit. He calls us to move from the known to the unknown of a new orientation to him.

Know that God remembers you. You are not forgotten. You are not alone.

Meditation: "He waited....Then he waited." (Genesis 8:10a, 12a)

Application: Consider the protections that you have constructed around yourself. How do you protect yourself? From what are you protecting yourself? Write down the thoughts that come to you. Examine this list.

Ask God to be your protector. Write down a list of steps you could take to move out of the self-protection that keeps you from God. Pray for the courage to take the first step. Post this list so that you can follow the steps as you wait for the waters to recede and for the land to be restored.

Prayer: Lord, I have been cooped up in my protective ark far too long. I know I must walk out into the open and move away from the protective shell that has encircled me. To walk out into the sunlight without that protective covering is frightening. In order to live life with the exuberance and vitality you developed in me, I know I have to trust in you. It is frightening to leave my protective shell where I have felt so safe and secure.

My fear is that if I do move outside of my protective ark, they will attack me. I do not know who "they" are, but my fear is real and powerful in a way that it is debilitating. Still, I want to be faithful, so I set before me doves that test the atmosphere outside of my ark of safety. Show me it is safe as you go before me preparing the way for new, everlasting life—life that is full and rich. Be my rock and my fortress. Comfort my soul, now and forever. In the name of Jesus, my Savior, I pray. Amen.

SECTION 3

Character Produces Hope

"God's end is to enable me to see
that he can walk on the chaos of my life just now."
—*Oswald Chambers*

DAY 27

Confusion and Peace

Scripture: I Corinthians 14:33a

> 33 For God is not a God of confusion but of peace.

Devotional Thoughts: Early in our marriage, Kathy and I lived in the mountains of North Carolina. We often hiked in those mountains with me leading the way. One of us would strap our son in a backpack and we would conquer the mountains nearby.

After an early start one Saturday, we arrived at the mountain we planned to climb that day. Since I had taught orienteering when I was in the Marine Corps, I kept the map and Kathy was satisfied to follow me.

We started on a broad, open trail. After a few hundred feet, the trail narrowed and continued narrowing as we climbed. Before long, we reached a fork in the trail and had to decide which direction to go. Neither path was worn enough to readily tell us to follow it, so I took out the map. We located ourselves and decided that the left fork was the correct one. After all, there was no creek on the map, but there was one ahead on the right.

We followed the left fork as it moved up the mountain. We hiked several switchbacks for awhile. Soon, however, the switchbacks ended and the trail went straight up the mountain. We had to push undergrowth out of our way as we climbed. With the sun getting hotter and hotter, we climbed straight up the steepest part of the mountain.

After awhile, Kathy decided to inform me that we were on the wrong trail. We both knew that the trail we had aimed for was heavily traveled. Thus, the heavy undergrowth and the briars grabbing our clothes would not be so thick if this trail was regularly traveled. Kathy became worried that we were lost, and I reassured her that we were not. She did not believe me, but had the presence of mind to keep her mouth shut.

Soon, there was no trail. We were faced with fallen logs, heavy tree cover, and thick undergrowth. We could not find any path in the immediate area. At this point, Kathy decided to inform me that we were definitely lost. I again reassured her we were not lost. She insisted that we were, but I pointed out that "up" would lead us to our original target—the top of the mountain.

We continued straight up. The tangled undergrowth and fallen logs had become a very steep climb. I knew, however, that "up" would lead us to the top of this mountain.

Before long, the trees broke away and a large mountain meadow spread out in front of us. The sky was incredibly clear and blue and the meadow was still and peaceful. The breeze that moved the meadow grass cooled us as we realized that we had reached the top of the mountain. As we looked around the meadow, we saw a group of hikers emerge from the actual trail, confirming that we, after all, had taken the wrong trail at the fork.

Often in our lives, we end up on a trail where it is difficult to see the way forward. At our feet is undergrowth that seems to hold us in its grip. We struggle to move through the denseness of it. At our body level are thorns and brambles that tear at our skin and cling to our clothes. Around us are dense forests that block our view. We find ourselves struggling to break through the confusion and chaos surrounding us.

We try to find our way through our disorienting surroundings. We try to see the path in front of us. Too often, we are unable to see our way out, so we just surrender to the chaos and confusion. Anxiety keeps us focused on the human perspective and it strangles our access to God's perspective.

Our God, however, is not a God of confusion. He is a God of peace. Paul reassures us of this fact in his first letter to the Corinthians. This reassurance is for us today as much as for the people of his day.

Just as we knew that "up" was the way to the top of the mountain, we can be assured that "up" is the way for us to direct ourselves when we are mired in hopelessness and confusion. God is there and listens to our pleas to be delivered from the chaos in our minds. He leads us upward toward him.

The second part of the verse, however, is the most powerful for those who are struggling with the confusion of posttraumatic stress and moral injury. If we focus on "up," then God will lead us to peace. We have to surrender to him and believe that he will lead us to the cool breezes that blow through the mountain meadows. He will lead us to peace.

God will not leave us or forsake us. He is the God of peace and he delivers that peace to us.

Meditation: "For God is not a God of confusion but of peace." (I Corinthians 14:33a)

Application: Imagine the struggles you are having as undergrowth and brambles. Imagine that you are climbing a mountain that leads you through those struggles. As you imagine this scene, imagine the "up" path that will lead you to peace. Ask God to help you climb the mountain through this undergrowth of confusion and chaos. Ask God for his peace to give you hope and calm your spirit. Believe that God will give you that hope.

Prayer: In your presence, Lord, I find peace, comfort, and security. That is where I long to be each day of my life. It is the essence of being in your company, where I can think and see clearly now the things that you would have me to experience. It is in your company that I find clearness of mind and all the confusion is taken away.

Lord, help me to rely on you in finding contentment in the places where confusion and despair seem to lurk. It is there I find you turning that disorder into a sense of order and calmness in my spirit. It is there, dear Father, that I find the courage to go on.

Peace, joy, and serenity—What blessings to experience! May each of my days be filled with these attributes of new life in you. For you are my God and are worthy to be praised. To your glory always, Father, I pray in your holy name. Amen

DAY 28

Finding Our Way Back

Scripture: Psalm 42:1–6

> 1 As a deer pants for flowing streams,
> so pants my soul for you, O God.
> 2 My soul thirsts for God,
> for the living God.
> When shall I come and appear before God?
> 3 My tears have been my food
> day and night,
> while they say to me all the day long,
> "Where is your God?"
> 4 These things I remember,
> as I pour out my soul:
> how I would go with the throng
> and lead them in procession to the house of God
> with glad shouts and songs of praise,
> a multitude keeping festival.
> 5 Why are you cast down, O my soul,
> and why are you in turmoil within me?
> Hope in God; for I shall again praise him,
> my salvation
> 6 and my God.

Devotional Thoughts: This Psalm conveys the plight of a man who, at one time, was the leader of the faithful on their way to the house of God. He would lead the songs and join in the music making. He praised God with a fervor unmatched by most.

At the time of this writing, however, the Psalmist's soul is "cast down." He longs for God like a deer longs for water. This Psalm reflects the spiritual experiences of traumatized people who encounter other people who scoff at their pain. The people ask the Psalmist, "Where is your God if you are suffering?" His tears are his food and his memories are painful. He has lost hope.

After I retired from the U.S. Navy as a chaplain, I began teaching at a small Christian university and in a men's program at a church. In both, I was a leader, but I was a leader hiding my traumatized spirit.

As time passed, I grew more confident in my relationships with the people so I shared my severe PTSD diagnosis. Many of their responses, like those in this Psalm, were to ask me the question that was haunting my spiritual life. The question was "How can you be a Christian and have PTSD?"

I was a Navy chaplain for more than twenty-six years. I had lead services all over the world—in Europe, in the Middle East, across the Pacific, in Africa, in Asia, and in the U.S. I had spent my career meeting the needs of those entrusted to me. I brought the light of God to them. Like the Psalmist, I was at the forefront of the throng that was worshipping.

I found myself thirsting for God's presence as a deer longs for water. No matter what I did, I was not able to reconnect with God. Christians around me were saying that I was the problem. I was the source of what was wrong with me. I was unable to find my way back. Like many traumatic survivors, I feared that those Christians were right.

Time passed and my soul remained cast down. I longed for God's love and presence. My spirit remained in turmoil. I was alone. I lost hope. I was overwhelmed with despair. I used this Psalm during this time of despair to remember, as the Psalmist did, what God had done for me in the past. I prayed that God would teach me to hope in him again. I told him that I longed to praise him and to thank him for my salvation. I prayed this prayer for several years.

As time passed, my spirit slowly healed. The Holy Spirit gradually led me through this time of disorientation. I found my way through the darkness and back to the light of God. I was again able to worship, but I worshipped with a deeper knowledge of God. I found a new orientation, one that was based on hope in God.

Many traumatized people find themselves on this same path. They once worshipped freely and gladly, but their lives have changed. They thirst for God and find themselves judged by many around them. This Psalm points the way for our spiritual journey—hope in God because you will again praise him. From the depths of despair, hope in God. He will not disappoint you.

This journey that I took from despair to hope is a journey on which the Holy Spirit leads Christians. Trauma—as I found out—is a path the Holy Spirit uses to draw us closer to God. In our modern world, trauma can be the only way that God can reach us. Realize that this journey is one that God requires so that we move deeper in relationship with him. Healing, hope, and peace wait at the end of this journey.

Meditation: "Hope in God." (Psalm 42:5b)

Application: Write out a prayer that follows the pattern of this Psalm. Include the ways that you were able to worship God in the past. Add the agony that you are now experiencing. End with a strong statement that God has been with you in the past and that you know he will be with you now and in the future. Pray this prayer when you are on the edge of despair.

Prayer: O Lord, my God, how my heart pants for you. I long for the streams of living water that quench the dryness of my soul. I long for the water that only comes from the loving touch of your presence. When I am in despair, all I can think of is the pain I am feeling and how your peace used to be part of my life before the trauma. So much of my energy is spent trying to understand what I did to get in this condition. These struggles lead to despair because I know I have drifted from a firm spiritual foundation.

Faithfulness to you—even when I do not have the energy—is what I pray for now. I pray for a deeper relationship with you that heals my spirit and soothes my soul. I pray for your revitalizing energy to fill me when I am weak. I pray for freedom from my despair. Send your Holy Spirit to fill me and to heal me.

Thank you, Lord, for your presence in my life that existed even when I thought all was dead and gone. As I place my hope in you, O God, I find a renewal deep in my spirit. Cause me to walk in your presence for the rest of my life. You are the stream of living water that quenches my thirst and soothes my soul. For that, I shall again praise you. In the name of our Lord, Jesus, who is my salvation and my God. Amen.

DAY 29

God's Promise of Presence

Scripture: Joshua 1:9

> 9 [God said,] "Have I not commanded you? Be strong and courageous. Do not be frightened, and do not be dismayed, for the LORD your God is with you wherever you go."

Devotional Thoughts: In *What It Is Like to Go to War,* Karl Marlantes describes his experiences in combat in Vietnam. He argues that combat has spiritual dimensions to it. After describing those dimensions, Marlantes states:

> The big difference is that the mystic sees heaven and the warrior sees hell....Many of us, including me, would *prefer* to think of a sacred space as some light-filled wondrous place where we can feel good and find a way to shore up our psyches against death. We don't want to think that something as ugly and brutal as combat could be involved in any way with the spiritual. However, would any practicing Christian say that Calvary Hill was not a sacred space? (2011, pp. 7–8).

Sacred spaces—places where we encounter God—can be the worst places on earth.

In Joshua 1, Moses has just died and God commands Joshua to lead the Israelites from their wilderness wanderings into the land that God had promised them. He instructs Joshua to be strong and courageous as they begin to conquer the Promised Land. Joshua shares these words with the Israelites.

The words, "Be strong and courageous," appear multiple times in this passage. The result of being strong and courageous is the knowledge that God is with the Israelites wherever they go. They are to be strong and courageous, and God promises to be present with them.

The interesting part of this command is that Joshua and his men are preparing for combat. They fight their way through the Promised Land in order to secure it as the nation of Israel. Thus, Marlantes concept of combat as a sacred space is illustrated by the stories of conquest that follow in the book of Joshua. God promises to be present with his people as they fight for the land.

In like manner, God promises to be with us as we struggle through the trauma of rape, abuse, combat, and their aftermath. No matter what caused the traumatic happenings, we, like Joshua, are to be "strong and courageous" in the knowledge that God is present with us. As we face the aftermath of trauma, we have God's promise to be with us.

The fear and dismay that follow traumatic experiences can leave us struggling with our daily lives. God gives us a simple command: Be strong and courageous. He instructs us not to be afraid or confused. We can know that he is with us wherever we go.

Marlantes reminds us that Jesus suffered through the trauma of the cross so that we can have a relationship with God. As we move toward healing from our traumatic wounds, be strong and courageous. Know that the Lord our God is with us wherever we go. Be secure in this knowledge.

Meditation: "The Lord your God is with you wherever you go." (Joshua 1:9b)

Application: What areas of your life are filled with fear and dismay? Make a list of these areas. Then ask God to help you be strong and courageous as you go through your day. Ask him to make you aware of his presence in your life.

Prayer: Sometimes, Lord, I just feel scared all over. I do not feel strength, power, or might in my body, mind, or spirit. I wonder if something is deeply wrong with me. Deep inside, I doubt everything.

Then, I remember the command you provided Joshua at just the right moment, reminding him that you would always be present with him. How empowering those words are to my soul. You said that you would never leave him or forsake him—ever! Then, O Lord, you provided powerful instructions when you told Joshua to avoid being terrified or dismayed. Instead, you told him to be strong and courageous because you would be with him wherever he went.

Thank you for those words that promised your presence to Joshua, but that also promise your presence to me today. You encourage me to rely on your strength and presence. Today, I can go on because of your presence, Lord, and because of your love for me. Bless your holy name forever and ever. Amen.

DAY 30

Returning to God

Scripture: Luke 15:17–24

> 17 “But when he came to himself, [the younger son] said,
> ‘How many of my father’s hired servants have more than
> enough bread, but I perish here with hunger! 18 I will
> arise and go to my father, and I will say to him, “Father,
> I have sinned against heaven and before you. 19 I am no
> longer worthy to be called your son. Treat me as one of
> your hired servants.”’ 20 And he arose and came to his
> father. But while he was still a long way off, his father saw
> him and felt compassion, and ran and embraced him
> and kissed him. 21 And the son said to him, ‘Father, I have
> sinned against heaven and before you. I am no longer
> worthy to be called your son.’ 22 But the father said to
> his servants, ‘Bring quickly the best robe, and put it on
> him, and put a ring on his hand, and shoes on his feet. 23
> And bring the fattened calf and kill it, and let us eat and
> celebrate. 24 For this my son was dead, and is alive again;
> he was lost, and is found.’ And they began to celebrate.”

Devotional Thoughts: Jesus told this story of the prodigal son to teach us of God’s love for us and acceptance of us even after we sin. In the first part of the story (Luke 15:1–16), the younger son demands his share of the inheritance so that he can make his own way in the world. His father gives the young man what he demands and then the son leaves. Demanding usually falls into the sin category. In this story, the young man should have waited to have his inheritance gifted to him by his father. Instead, he demands what "is his"—though technically, all of the items still belong to his father.

With the large sum in his pocket, the son makes many new friends and pays for many pleasures in life. He enters a life that is far from the one he had at home. He drinks, gambles, womanizes, and enjoys all of the things that money can purchase. The young man fails to notice how far into sin he has gone.

One day, the money runs out and so does the loyalty of his new friends. As time passes, the young man finds himself deeper and deeper in poverty. This decline culminates when he is with pigs, hoping to be able to eat a bit of the food he is feeding them. Pigs, to the Jews of that day, were the ultimate filthy animals. Pigs were "unclean" and thus, the young man broke yet another rule of his faith. This young man is starving and "unclean" (in a spiritual sense) when a thought comes to him.

The scripture passage begins with this awareness from the young man. No servant in his father's house is hungry or filthy and no one has to compromise religious beliefs to work in his father's house. The young man decides to go home, ask for forgiveness, and beg for a job at his father's house. The young man has become aware of the plight that his sinful lifestyle has left him in. He determines to ask forgiveness and take his place at the lowliest part of his father's household.

In like manner, we have to become aware of the sin in our lives. In our responses to trauma, we often can commit sins that we know about and sins that we do not know about. As the Apostle Paul states, we all have sinned and fallen short of the glory of God (Romans 3:23). Becoming aware of the sin that is separating us from God is essential to repairing our relationship with him. We, too, need to approach our Father in heaven to ask for forgiveness.

Understanding how God will greet us is the main point of Jesus' parable. Jesus explains that as the young man approaches the house—he is still far away—his father sees him and runs to him. The father feels compassion for his son, embracing and kissing him. The father must have spent most of his days faithfully watching for his younger son to return home. The father opens his arms and embraces his son.

The son attempts his prepared speech of asking to be a servant, but the father brushes it all away. He is overjoyed to have his son home. The father instructs the servants to prepare a magnificent feast. He says, "For this my son was dead, and is alive again; he was lost, and is found" (v 24).

This story speaks to those of us who have decided that what they have done is far worse than God can ever forgive. When we feel that we are too sinful or "bad" to pray to God, we miss the welcome that God extends to us, his children. Just as this father watched daily for his child to return, God waits for us to come to him.

When we do approach God, he throws his arms around us and welcomes us. He forgives us for what we have done and welcomes us back home. We, however, have to look around us at the life we are living—filled with despair, self-hatred, and shame—and decide to begin the journey to God.

We can be assured of God's forgiveness when we confess our sins to him. He will always forgive us and welcome us home. He is waiting for you today.

Meditation: "For this my son was dead, and is alive again; he was lost, and is found." (Luke 15:24)

Application: Reread the scripture for today. Imagine the journey home that the son began in shame and guilt and finished with love and forgiveness.

Now, imagine that you are the son entrenched in guilt, shame, and sin. Look around you at your situation and realize that God is waiting and watching for you to begin your journey to him. Ask God for forgiveness for your sins and begin your journey homeward to God. Believe that he waits for you with love and forgiveness.

Prayer: Lord, do you remember when I said: "Just give me what is mine, Father, so I can go on my own way?" As always, however, you were faithful to me through the whole ordeal. You allowed me to take matters into my own hand, make my own sinful decisions, and become just the opposite of the person you created me to be. You allowed this even when you knew it would cause me great distress and pain. In despair, I realized my own shortcomings and the ways I have sinned against you and you only. How can you ever receive and love me as your own once again?

For my arrogance, pride, and conceitedness, O Lord, I humbly come before you and ask for your forgiveness. O God, there is nothing like the open, welcoming arms of a forgiving and loving Father. Even when I do not deserve your love, you love me with a ferocity that is refreshing, cleansing, and restoring. You receive me once again as your very own cherished one. How powerful is your grace. Thank you, Heavenly Father, for forgiving me and giving me new life. Today is the day you have made and you are greatly to be praised for it. May your name be exalted forevermore, Lord Jesus. Amen.

DAY 31

Pray Without Ceasing

Scripture: I Thessalonians 5:16–18

> 16 Rejoice always, 17 pray without ceasing, 18 give thanks in all circumstances; for this is the will of God in Christ Jesus for you.

Devotional Thoughts: In Matthew 6:9–13, Jesus addresses the crowds gathered to hear his teachings in the passage that we term, "The Sermon on the Mount." Jesus gives instructions on prayer, ending with what we call "The Lord's Prayer." He states:

> 9 Pray then like this:
> "Our Father in heaven,
> hallowed be your name.
> 10 Your kingdom come,
> your will be done,
> on earth as it is in heaven.
> 11 Give us this day our daily bread,
> 12 and forgive us our debts,
> as we also have forgiven our debtors.
> 13 And lead us not into temptation,
> but deliver us from evil.

This prayer is often part of our worship services. It also has much meaning for us as we seek our way out of trauma's hold.

The first concept is that we should pray. Jesus commands us to pray. It is not a recommendation. When we are in the grips of spiritual injury or posttraumatic stress, we can feel that God is not listening to us, and that we are alone with little to no contact with God. At these times, we must read this scripture and know that Jesus commanded us to pray. Then, if necessary, we go through the motions of prayer, having faith that God is hearing us. If we record our prayers, then we can look back to see how God was working in our lives, even when we were unaware of that work.

In I Thessalonians 5, Paul instructs us to "pray without ceasing." Rejoicing, praying, and giving thanks are God's will for us according to these verses. These practices will build endurance in our spirits which will lead us to hope. The Lord's Prayer has these elements in it, but we can be confused about how to broaden our prayers. John Stott, a British theologian, provides several types of prayer that assist us in understanding various ways to approach God in prayer.

Stott describes five ways that we can pray that allow us to learn to "pray without ceasing." These five kinds of prayer imitate the sections of the Lord's Prayer that Jesus taught us to pray. These kinds of prayers help us to focus on different attitudes of prayer. They are as follows:

1. **Look up to God.** This involves worship where we give God the glory due him. We praise God for what he has done in our lives and in our world. Keep a list of the times in a day that you experience the wonder of God's actions or of his kingdom. This could be in nature such as a sunset or it could be in a relationship when someone stopped for a moment to speak with you and that was just what you needed at that moment. Praise God for working in this world and your life.

Jesus teaches us to look up to God in these words: "Our Father in heaven, hallowed be your name. Your kingdom come, your will be done, on earth as it is in heaven" (verses 9b-10). Through these words, we give God the glory that is due him. We acknowledge God as holy and we ask that his will be done throughout creation.

2. **Look within yourself.** This type of prayer can be the most difficult for the traumatized soul. Often, after we experience traumatic events, we feel a deep sense of shame and guilt. We feel that we are not worthy of God's help. Looking within ourselves to confess honestly the sins that we have committed brings healing in small steps. Important to this kind of prayer is confession of our sins, followed by thanking God for his forgiveness. Accepting forgiveness can be a challenge for traumatized spirits.

   In the Lord's Prayer, Jesus addresses our look inward by focusing on asking for forgiveness from sin (v. 12) and for the power to avoid temptation with deliverance from evil (v. 13). All of these concepts are necessary to help us learn to depend on God for our moment-to-moment and day-to-day lives.

3. **Look around at your family and friends.** Focusing on the needs of others can help us move out of the self-protective stance that can be a part of traumatization. If we begin a list of the needs of others and spend time in prayer being as specific and concrete as possible, then we begin to move out of ourselves and into concern for the needs of others. This type of prayer is also called "intercession."

   Jesus introduces prayer for others with "Your kingdom come, your will be done, on earth as it is in heaven." While not praying directly for certain people, Jesus instead prays for all people on earth. He asks God to do the best action possible—impose his will on earth like it is in heaven. Thus, Jesus prays that the perfection that is in heaven will be on earth as well.

4. **Look back at the past.** Give thanks to God for his goodness to you. Remembering his works in our lives and in the lives around us helps us begin to focus outward. We can also understand how God was with us, even when we were in the dark places. Again, a list of these memories will allow you to thank God for what he has done for you and for others. The list will also help you avoid temptation and evil in the future—if you ask for God's help.

   "And lead us not into temptation, but deliver us from evil" are the words that Jesus uses to focus on both the past and future. We have been tempted and we have participated in evil. Much of the guilt and shame that traumatized people feel is from actions where they participated in what they perceived was evil. This guilt and shame are major parts of spiritual injury. Jesus asks God to help us look back at the past in order to help us avoid such actions in the future.

5. **Look forward to the future.** Looking forward to the future means that we offer prayers and petitions of request to God regarding our own needs. The guilt, shame, and horror that erupt from our traumatic experiences are items to take to God in prayer. He cares that we are suffering and he will comfort us. Make a list of the requests you have for God and pray that he will act in your life.

   In verse 11, Jesus teaches us to ask for our daily bread—not weekly, monthly, or yearly—but daily bread. Asking God to help us through this day is a lesson from Jesus. Our future can extend past this day, but our needs are limited to the present. Ask God to help you understand what your needs are that are aligned with his will. Pray for those needs.

When we pray without ceasing, we learn to live our lives in an attitude of prayer. In some prayers, we are thankful and we praise God. In some prayers, we confess our sins and accept his forgiveness. In other prayers, we ask him to intercede with family, friends, or ourselves. As we go through our daily routines, we should pray constantly so that we develop an attitude of prayer. Through prayer, we can receive healing.

Meditation: "Pray without ceasing." (I Thessalonians 5:17)

Application: Consider Stott's five types of prayers. Which one do you consider the easiest kind to pray? Make a list of the items you could pray for and begin a time of prayer each day. After a few days, add another kind of prayer by making a list and beginning to pray for the items on that list. Every few days, create a list for a different kind of prayer.

As you move through your days, repeat prayers for the people or events that are on the list as you remember them. Soon, you will find that you are "praying without ceasing" throughout your day as you pray for items on your list.

Prayer: Speaking to you, Lord, refreshes me. For in talking with you, I find presence, a real incarnational presence. I feel your presence in me as I feel the Holy Spirit comfort me. I know that I am on holy ground.

Through your Spirit, O Lord, give me words to speak as I try to express my feelings about you. Help me to know what petitions to place before you. In doing this, calm my soul and give me peace as I walk in your presence. Thank you, Lord, for hearing my prayers. In your hallowed name I offer this prayer. Amen.

DAY 32

Rest for the Weary

Scripture: Matthew 11:28–30

> 28 [Jesus said] "Come to me, all who labor and are heavy
> laden, and I will give you rest. 29 Take my yoke upon you,
> and learn from me, for I am gentle and lowly in heart,
> and you will find rest for your souls. 30 For my yoke is
> easy, and my burden is light."

Devotional Thoughts: Farmers in Biblical times used a yoke with their plowing. The yoke was a large piece of wood that usually fit across the shoulders of two oxen. When yoked together, the oxen were able to pull the plow through the fields, creating rows for planting.

The yoke kept the oxen together, but also allowed the farmer to control the oxen's movements. With a yoke, the oxen moved together to accomplish the tasks that the farmer set before them. The farmer completed his work each day—his labors—by yoking his oxen and guiding them through the fields.

The yokes, large pieces of wood, were heavy on the animals' necks. In order for the yoke to fit correctly, two oxen had to be about the same size. The workday for the oxen involved being yoked together as they pulled the plow around the fields.

When we experience trauma, we can become yoked with the traumatic memories and emotions so that we only complete our daily tasks by working alongside the trauma. This yoke of trauma weighs us down so that our days become a blur of depression and weariness. We often feel that the yoke is too heavy to carry, the burden too overwhelming. Yet, we lack a way to free ourselves from this yoke of traumatic wounding.

Jesus addresses yokes and burdens in this passage. He uses this concept of a yoke to explain his presence in our lives, especially when the load becomes too heavy. The fact that Jesus addresses this issue shows us that God is aware of our difficult times and that he is aware that some experiences in our lives are beyond our abilities to cope.

Jesus offers his yoke to us…an exchange of yokes. We are to approach him when we labor and are heavy laden. Referring to a heavy load, "heavy laden" can be the incredible load we bear when we are traumatized by events in our lives. Nightmares, horrific memories, guilt, shame, and depression can weigh on us as a heavy yoke.

At times, we experience Jesus' yoke through another person. That person is yoked to us to walk beside us as we walk through the terrors and horrors that stalk us. Jesus sends his followers to us to give us comfort and guidance.

Inviting us to learn from him, Jesus says that he is "gentle" and "lowly in heart." When depression, nightmares, and terrors from the past are our constant companions, the invitation to experience "gentleness" can be beyond our comprehension.

By exchanging yokes—trauma for gentleness—we can experience a yoke that is easy and a burden that is light. By turning to Jesus and exchanging yokes, "you will find rest for your souls." Rest is a promise from Jesus.

Meditation: "You will find rest for your souls." (Matthew 11:29b)

Application: Feel the yoke that you are bearing at this time. Write down what items are making this load so heavy. One by one, surrender each item to Jesus. Ask for his yoke and for his gentleness. Ask Jesus to give you rest for your soul and ask him for a friend to walk through this traumatic wound with you.

Prayer: Lord Jesus, the yoke of past trauma has weighed heavy on my soul. Carrying that load of shame, guilt, depression, nightmares, terrors, the inner pain that comes from letting you and others down, the embarrassment of failing, and becoming emotionally wounded is sometimes too heavy to bear. My body becomes weary from the emotional load that I carry. Sometimes I just want to quit. Rest…rest if what I need!

Father, I come to you asking for relief from the load I bear. I come to you heavy laden looking for rest. Take my yoke, O Lord, and make my burden light. Help me to find my rest in you. Heal my brokenness and give me new life that can only be found in you. For you are my God and Savior. You are my great Redeemer, my Healer, and my Comforter. I will praise you all the days of my life. Amen.

DAY 33

Forgiveness for Sins

Scripture: Psalm 51:7–12

7 Purge me with hyssop, and I shall be clean;
wash me, and I shall be whiter than snow.
8 Let me hear joy and gladness;
let the bones that you have broken rejoice.
9 Hide your face from my sins,
and blot out all my iniquities.
10 Create in me a clean heart, O God,
and renew a right spirit within me.
11 Cast me not away from your presence,
and take not your Holy Spirit from me.
12 Restore to me the joy of your salvation,
and uphold me with a willing spirit.

Devotional Thoughts: "How can I live with what I did?" is a recurrent question of warriors when they return from combat. This question is also one that many victims of trauma ask as they question why they did not do this or why they did do that. These questions haunt trauma victims, causing them to feel deep shame and isolation.

In II Samuel 11–12, King David participates in several incidents that lead him far from the path of God. The first verse of these chapters explains that spring is the time of year when kings go to war. As the king of Israel, David's role was to lead his men in battle; yet, David was in Jerusalem. This key to the story shows that David was not fulfilling the responsibilities that God had given him.

What follows is a rapid downhill slide for David. He spots a woman bathing on a nearby roof, finds out she is someone else's wife, and has her brought to him anyway. He sleeps with her, she becomes pregnant, and then David attempts to cover-up the pregnancy. Misusing his kingly authority, David orders the husband home to sleep with his wife in order to cover-up the adultery.

The husband, desiring to remain holy for battle, does not sleep with his wife. David orders the man's death when he returns to battle. David then takes the new widow as his wife. When confronted by Nathan the prophet, David refuses to acknowledge his sin. Through a story that Nathan tells, David finally realizes how much he had moved into the murky world of sin.

Thus, David committed adultery, tried to cover it up, ordered the murder of the husband, married the widow to cover up the pregnancy, and finally refused to acknowledge his waywardness from God's way. Once David listened to Nathan, David realized his sin and cried out to God for forgiveness.

God called David "a man after my own heart;" yet, David was able to wander this far from God's way. Deeply mired in sin, it would seem that David had broken his relationship with God beyond repair.

"How can I live with what I did?" is a question that David could easily have asked. Yet, David asked God for forgiveness and received it. Psalm 51 records the words that David used as he sought forgiveness for his sins. God forgave David and God forgives us.

David prays to God for cleansing from sin. David asks God to hide his sins from God's face so that God no longer remembers them. Creating a new heart and renewing a right spirit is David's request, and it can also be our request.

God can cleanse us from the guilt and shame that our actions can bring. He can create a new heart within us and return a spirit that is in line with him. We just have to ask him for forgiveness and cleansing.

Meditation: "Create in me a clean heart, O God, and renew a right spirit within me." (Psalm 51:10)

Application: Take quiet time to lay out before God the shame and guilt you feel for your actions. Acknowledge that God can forgive you. Ask him for forgiveness and then ask him to create a new heart and a clean spirit within you.

When you feel the guilt and shame, remember this time of forgiveness. Thank God for forgiving you and cleansing you.

Prayer: I call upon you, Jesus, for you are the Christ, the Son of the living God. It is in you that I find cleansing from the iniquities and sins of life. I want to hide from you, but it is by facing my shortcomings that I am able to confess them to you. I know I must stand before you completely exposed in confession before I can experience the freeing power of your mercy.

Where guilt once reigned and had power over me, your cleansing grace has delivered to me a new heart that seeks you with a new passion and commitment. May I never forget the loving forgiveness provided by the cross and the sacrifices that you experienced for me. Let me feel free of these burdens that I have carried too long. Through Jesus, my Lord, I offer this prayer. Amen.

DAY 34

Healing

Scripture: John 5:1–9

> [1] After this there was a feast of the Jews, and Jesus went
> up to Jerusalem. [2] Now there is in Jerusalem by the
> Sheep Gate a pool, in Aramaic called Bethesda, which
> has five roofed colonnades. [3] In these lay a multitude
> of invalids—blind, lame, and paralyzed—waiting for the
> moving of the water; [4] for an angel of the Lord went
> down at certain seasons into the pool, and stirred the
> water: whoever stepped in first after the stirring of the
> water was healed of whatever disease he had. [5] One man
> was there who had been an invalid for thirty-eight years.
> [6] When Jesus saw him lying there and knew that he had
> already been there a long time, he said to him, "Do you
> want to be healed?" [7] The sick man answered him, "Sir,
> I have no one to put me into the pool when the water
> is stirred up, and while I am going another steps down
> before me." [8] Jesus said to him, "Get up, take up your
> bed, and walk." [9] And at once the man was healed, and
> he took up his bed and walked.

Devotional Thoughts: One of the problems with experiencing trauma is that often people who were not with you at the time, do not "get it." Warriors return from the combat zone feeling out of step with family and friends back home. Other traumatic experiences change our view of the world. As a result of trauma, our lives change drastically so that we can feel out of step with family and friends.

Many churches today tend to focus on the positives in life and tend to block out the difficult recoveries from trauma. When we are mired in the depths of traumatic wounding, we are much like this man who had been an invalid for thirty-eight years.

Day after day, this man had remained by this pool of water, waiting to be healed. He had great faith in the healing power of this water. His problem, however, was that each time he attempted to reach the water, someone beat him to it. He had no one to help him.

When our soul is deeply wounded from what we have seen, smelled, and experienced through trauma, oftentimes all we can do is lay beside the water. We go to church, incapable of moving ourselves to a place of healing. Oftentimes, it feels as if no one is there to help us. The gap between the traumatized and the healthy can seem insurmountable.

This man, however, shows great faith. He is there by the pool daily with the hope of making it to the water for healing. He has not given up hope. He does not despair.

Jesus sees the man lying beside the water. The first question Jesus asks is: "Do you want to be healed?" While seemingly an obvious question—after all, the man is there daily hoping to be healed—Jesus still has the man answer the question. Jesus is ascertaining the man's true desires, the desires of his heart.

The man answers Jesus with his needs. The man cannot rapidly enter the water and he has no one to help him. Without the help of another person, the man is too slow to be able to receive healing. Yet, the man comes back day after day for the possibility of healing.

Jesus tells the man to get up, take his bed, and walk. The man is healed.

Sometimes we feel like the man who sat by the water, waiting to be healed. It seems as if Christians around us are always able to enter the water before us. They tell us their stories of how God worked in their lives and how they were healed. We long to feel that healing to be free from the terrors of the night and the flashbacks of the day. Our traumatized spirits long for the healing that is possible; yet, we can be too slow to enter the healing water.

This story tells us that we must continue to have faith that we will be healed. Just as this man went day after day, year after year, to the pool for healing, we must continue to go to God to ask for healing.

This man needed another person to help him heal. Many studies advocate having the help of someone who has already been down the road of trauma that we are traveling. Jesus helped the man; yet, he became so much more to the man.

Jesus reveals himself as the Son of God when he heals the man's lifelong physical challenge. Healing is available for wounds to the spirit as well. Jesus is the healer of our spirits as we fight to overcome the adverse effects of traumatic wounds.

Follow the example of this man at the pool. Go to church to be faithful. Find a friend who can help you. Turn to Jesus for healing of your spirit. Believe that he will heal your wounded spirit.

Meditation: [Jesus asked], "Do you want to be healed?" (John 5:6b)

Application: Who are people in your life who can help you walk the path to healing your spiritual wound? Make a list and ask God to lead you to someone who can walk with you. Contact these people to ask them for help. Do not be discouraged if they say "no" to this request. Be faithful like the man in the story. Continue searching.

Continue worshipping and seeking Jesus. Ask for healing. Realize that at times, healing is a rapid process, and at times, healing is a slow process.

Prayer: Yes, Lord Jesus, I want to be healed! I do not know how many times I have said that Lord. It was as if I was just saying it and not believing it enough to move. You opened my eyes to the people you have sent to walk with me, to guide me through this healing process. Someone who holds me accountable. Someone who cares for and loves me enough to provide encouragement. Someone who has the ability to call me out of my own self-pity and dejectedness.

Lord Jesus, once again, your Spirit worked through the one you sent to guide, encourage, and help me work through the wound to my inner being. You call on me to get up and walk, to move forward, to accept the reality that had already taken place in my body, mind, and spirit. You called me out of depression and despair.

You gave me something to live for which is a deeper relationship with you because you gave me hope for tomorrow. And for that, Lord, I am eternally grateful. For you are the Lord, my God, the healer of my soul, and for that, I will praise you all the day and night. Through Jesus, my Savior, I pray. Amen.

DAY 35

Trust and Hope

Scripture: Matthew 14:22–33

> [22] Immediately [Jesus] made the disciples get into the boat and go before him to the other side, while he dismissed the crowds. [23] And after he had dismissed the crowds, he went up on the mountain by himself to pray. When evening came, he was there alone, [24] but the boat by this time was a long way from the land, beaten by the waves, for the wind was against them. [25] And in the fourth watch of the night he came to them, walking on the sea. [26] But when the disciples saw him walking on the sea, they were terrified, and said, "It is a ghost!" and they cried out in fear.
>
> [27] But immediately Jesus spoke to them, saying, "Take heart; it is I. Do not be afraid." [28] And Peter answered him, "Lord, if it is you, command me to come to you on the water." [29] He said, "Come." So Peter got out of the boat and walked on the water and came to Jesus. [30] But when he saw the wind, he was afraid, and beginning to sink he cried out, "Lord, save me." [31] Jesus immediately reached out his hand and took hold of him, saying to him, "O you of little faith, why did you doubt?" [32] And when they got into the boat, the wind ceased. [33] And

those in the boat worshiped him, saying, "Truly you are the Son of God."

Devotional Thoughts: After a long day with crowds of people, Jesus went by himself to pray. When evening came, he encouraged his disciples to leave ahead of him. They left, sailing their boat across the Sea of Galilee.

The disciples were struggling to make progress because the wind was so strong. At some time between 3 am and 6 am, they saw what they thought was a ghost walking on the water toward them.

When Jesus heard them, he identified himself and told them not to be afraid. Peter's response was one that asked for proof. He asked Jesus to let him walk on the water as well.

Peter's response offers several layers for understanding. First, Peter believes that Jesus is able to walk on water. Peter never questions whether Jesus has the ability to allow him to walk on water. Next, Peter just gets straight out of the boat and is on the water when Jesus says, "Come." Peter exhibits extreme faith with his response of getting out of the boat in the middle of a strong wind that was producing a perilous sea and was preventing their boat from making good progress.

Peter gets out of the boat and walks on the water! This act is an incredible happening, which proves not only Jesus' identity, but also Jesus' power. Peter's response is equally amazing as he—without hesitating—goes straight into the water and walks on it.

Suddenly, however, Peter looks away from Jesus and realizes where he is and what is happening. Fear prevented Peter from continuing in his faith journey to Jesus. Peter became afraid of the wind. This fear caused Peter to begin to sink.

Yet, Peter's faith is still strong amidst his fear. He immediately calls out to Jesus, "Lord, save me." Jesus reaches out and rescues Peter with an admonition of "O you of little faith, why did you doubt?" When they both are on the boat, the wind stops.

Peter gives in to his fear, which causes him to sink. Jesus responds immediately to Peter when Peter asks for help. Peter's initial faith instantly changes to fear. Remembering that Peter is a fisherman by profession helps us know that the winds must have been very strong for Peter to be afraid of them.

Fear separated Peter from Jesus. When we experience traumatic events in our lives, our spirits are wounded. Oftentimes, we become consumed by fear (if we are honest with ourselves). Fear can become the controller of our lives during times of disorientation.

By allowing fear to control us, we no longer allow God to control us. We want to protect ourselves but, as Peter demonstrates, we often sink deeper into the stormy sea when fear consumes us. Disorientation rules us.

This story, however, is one of hope. Even though he loses faith for a moment, Peter cries out to Jesus and Jesus rescues him. The wind calms. The disciples know that they have been in the presence of the Son of God. They have a new appreciation of the power of Jesus.

Many of us have a relationship with Jesus. We worship him and we know of his power on earth. There are times in our lives, when we set sail in a boat that enters stormy waters. These storms can be nightmares, trauma, flashbacks, and other ways that instill fear inside of us. In this time of disorientation, what we thought we knew about our relationship with God, with others, and with life is turned upside down.

Jesus calls us to come to him. He knows that we are in the storm. He wants us to trust him and to step out toward him when he calls to us. The problem is that we have to step out into the storm that we fear. Our fears battle the voice of Jesus.

The hope within this situation is that we have to have Peter's faith—the faith to step out on the water toward Jesus. We know that if we do allow our fear to get the best of us, Jesus will answer us and rescue us as he did with Peter.

In stepping into the stormy wind and in knowing that Jesus will respond if we lose focus, we learn about Jesus. Just as the disciples came to know him in a different way because of this incident, we can also know Jesus and God in a different way. We can learn a new orientation that restores hope and faith in God our Father, Jesus his Son, and the Holy Spirit our Comforter.

Meditation: Jesus [said], "O you of little faith, why did you doubt?" (Matthew 14:31)

Application: Imagine that you are in that boat on the stormy sea. What is the storm for you? Think of the items that cause you fear. Be still and listen to the voice of Jesus calling you to step out into that storm and to have faith that he will save you. Do this each day until you can step out of the boat and walk toward Jesus. Trust him to conquer the winds that are blowing you about and to calm your spirit.

Prayer: Come, Lord Jesus, and be my hope! Let me know you are by my side. At times, my sense of self is rocked by my woundedness. It is as if I cannot stand, as if I am all alone. I find myself walking in fear, wondering if hope exists.

Then I remember your Word, how life changing and exacting it is. How powerful is your Word, O Lord. It continues to call life into being. It provides courage and faithfulness even when I do not feel those attributes. It is the essence and reality of hope!

Be my strength O Lord. Lift my countenance. Calm my fears. Cause me to walk with your energy, which renews my soul. For I know that you, Heavenly Father, are always there, ready to respond when I call to you. Even when I cannot feel or see your presence, you are there. In that presence, I am lifted up and encouraged.

Today, O Lord, I walk in peace, having known again and again your loving existence by my side. Thank you for walking with me through the trials of this day. In the name above all other names, Jesus Christ, I pray. Amen.

SECTION 4

Hope Does Not Put Us to Shame

"Leave the broken, irreversible past in God's hands, and step out into the invincible future with him."
—*Oswald Chambers*

DAY 36

The Secret of Strength

Scripture: Philippians 4:11–13

> [11] Not that I am speaking of being in need, for I have
> learned in whatever situation I am to be content. [12] I
> know how to be brought low, and I know how to abound.
> In any and every circumstance, I have learned the secret
> of facing plenty and hunger, abundance and need. [13] I
> can do all things through him who strengthens me.

Devotional Thoughts: In this passage, Paul tells the Philippians that he has learned how to find contentment through God in all circumstances of his life. He has learned to turn to God for strength and thus, find contentment. Paul did not turn to God to change his situations, but, instead, he turned to God to give him strength for whatever situation he found himself.

On December 8, 1941, the Japanese began an air campaign in the Philippines where United States troops were stationed. The battle continued for about five months before the Japanese were able to seize all the islands in the Philippines.

At the time, seventy-seven women were serving as nurses for the Army and Navy at Bataan, Corregidor, and several other duty stations. These nurses, for the most part, had agreed to accept the assignment to the Philippines because of the atmosphere of fun and adventure that was part of the job. December 8, however, changed the lives of these women forever.

For the five months that Japan was attacking, the nurses cared for the injured. As the Americans continued to pull in their perimeter, the nurses moved with them. They protected the wounded and worked long hours trying to save lives.

Then in April 1942, the Philippines fell to Japan. The seventy-seven nurses became prisoners of war. They faced hunger bordering on starvation, diseases and infections, insects and poisonous creatures, and other extreme conditions that prisoners of war (POW) face in enemy-held lands.

The nurses kept to a rigid schedule of treating the starving and sick even though they, too, were starving. They used the discipline that the military had instilled in them to hold on to the hope that their situation would change. That one day, they would again be free.

In January 1945, the Allies reclaimed the Philippines from Japan. The nurses were freed from the POW camp. Somehow, all seventy-seven of them had survived the horrendous conditions in the camp. These women had not only survived, but all of them were still nursing at the time they were freed. The disciplines that had served them well in military life, also served them well in the POW camp. They found strength to survive because of the disciplines of their lives.

When these courageous seventy-seven nurses returned to the U.S., they were instructed to keep the horror of their experiences to themselves. America, according to those in charge, was not ready to hear how women had been treated in the POW camp. These brave nurses could not share their stories and, instead, had to begin living their lives pretending to be fine.

Thus, the women's bravery and courage under the most traumatic circumstances had to be hidden. The women moved on with their lives, accepting the orders to remain quiet about the terrors of their time in the Philippines. They drew on the strength that they had relied on in the attacks and in the camps to face this new challenge—society's refusal to acknowledge their sacrifices and their contribution to the war.

The war experiences and the post-war experiences for these seventy-seven nurses were traumatic. Yet, they found the strength to cling to the hope that they would return to the U.S. and that they would one day tell their stories.

In like manner, we have the example of Paul. Like the nurses, he went through a daily disciplined exercise to keep his strength. He daily focused on God through prayer and the study of scripture. Paul, no matter the circumstances of his life, turned to God for strength. In that strength, he found contentment. His circumstances were not changed by God, but Paul's heart was content.

The secret of gaining the strength needed to face the difficulties that trauma brings to our lives is to maintain the spiritual disciplines of our lives. Even if we are in a time of hunger and need, we need to maintain our daily scripture reading and prayer time.

The discipline of going to God through prayer and scripture reading—no matter the circumstances of our lives—allows God to interact with us. God will fill us with strength though it may not be in the moment we choose. But God will deliver us.

Hope in the strength that comes from our Father in heaven. He will bring contentment to our lives if we allow him to strengthen us.

Meditation: "I can do all things through him [Christ] who strengthens me." (Philippians 4:13)

Application: How does God strengthen you daily? Can you allow him to strengthen you? Make a commitment to begin praying each day and reading the Bible. In that time, stay open before God and ask him for strength to move through the period of disorientation so that you can find hope through a new orientation to him.

Prayer: Sometimes, Lord, we just want to scream out and tell the world of the injustices that we are experiencing. Life is difficult enough as it is without being mistreated by others, enduring the injustice of being fired, or hearing the untimely diagnosis of cancer. Even in overcoming these struggles, we know the key is to keep our eyes focused on you, Lord God.

There are times when we just go through our days without making much of our troubles. The pain is still there, but somehow we continue to go on. O God, we go on because it is in you that we find strength to be a witness, to be able to bear the truth, and to walk with a sense of purpose again. Although we can still fall into moments of despair and discouragement, Father, we realize that it is more courageous and obedient to call on you to provide the strength to stand tall in the midst of our inner struggles.

Calling on you, O Lord, gives us strength and hope because we know you will always answer our prayers. You stand with us, undergirding us with your presence and affirmation. We are assured that you will always be with us, comforting us wherever we go. We are forever reminded that we can do all things through you who strengthens us. We are blessed beyond measure. Our cup runneth over, and we will dwell in the house of the Lord evermore. Praise be to your name forever, dear Lord. Amen.

DAY 37

New Orientation

Scripture: Psalm 23

> 1 The LORD is my shepherd;
> I shall not want.
> 2 He makes me lie down in green pastures.
> He leads me beside still waters.
> 3 He restores my soul.
> He leads me in paths of righteousness for his name's sake.
> 4 Even though I walk through the valley of the shadow of death,
> I will fear no evil, for you are with me;
> your rod and your staff, they comfort me.
> 5 You prepare a table before me in the presence of my enemies;
> you anoint my head with oil; my cup overflows.
> 6 Surely goodness and mercy shall follow me all the days of
> my life,
> and I shall dwell in the house of the LORD forever.

Devotional Thoughts: Sheep and shepherds are not part of most of our lives. Yet, when our family lived in Iceland, we saw many sheep as we drove around the island. There were few fences to limit the sheep's movements. Since wool sweaters and other woolen products are a major part of the economy in Iceland, law-makers have passed laws to protect the sheep and the farmers' investments. If a motorist runs over a sheep, then the motorist owes the farmer for the loss. The penalties include paying for that sheep, its possible children, and its possible grandchildren.

This legal situation led sheep to stand passively in the middle of the road as cars swerved to miss them. Oftentimes, the sheep would lie in wait until a car was about to pass them. Then the sheep would leap into the road in front of a car, causing the driver to slam on brakes. Many people on base reported "near misses" with sheep. Going out into the countryside often seemed like courting financial disaster.

When we have times of trials and testing (as the Bible terms them), we cry out to God. He responds by providing for us with times of plenty and calmness. Sheep need green pastures for food and still waters for drink. Our Shepherd provides for us so that our needs are met. God also leads us in the paths of righteousness so that we understand his goodness. This existence is termed, "orientation," by Walter Brueggemann (2002, p. x). This term can be interchanged with the term, "normal."

However, when we "walk through the valley of the shadow of death," we can feel that God is not there. We can form the belief that God no longer cares for us. This period of "disorientation" (Brueggemann, 2002, p. x) is a time when we lose control in our lives and we are traumatized. This Psalm of David brings assurance to us that God is with us and we do not need to fear the evil that we face. God's presence is there. But his presence is described as a "rod and staff." These items are instruments that shepherd's use to prod sheep into movement or into returning to the flock. When we enter periods of disorientation, we enter a time when God deepens our knowledge of him and he prods us into a new understanding of his presence in our lives. He moves us to a "new orientation," (Brueggemann, 2002, p. x) a time when we have a new understanding of God and his work in our lives.

The next section of this Psalm is a disturbing one. In this period of "new orientation," God places a table before us in the presence of our enemies. The power of this verse for traumatized people is that we do not have to be healed for God to work in our lives. In the midst of our "enemies"—nightmares, flashbacks, terrors, etc.—God comes to us and anoints us with oil. His blessings overflow through our lives. Understanding that God uses his rod and staff to prod us into a deeper relationship with him as we journey through life leads us to a new understanding (new orientation) of God and his work among us.

Our Father in heaven will restore our souls if we journey with him through our wounds. He will move us from disorientation to a new orientation in our relationship with him. Turn to him and let him begin to lead you to a new orientation that can restore your soul.

Meditation: "He restores my soul." (Psalm 23:3)

Application: List your "enemies" that plague your life each day. Study the list. Then ask God to prepare a table for you so that you can know his presence in the midst of your enemies.

Be still and know that God is restoring your soul.

Prayer: O Father, as the shepherd cares for his sheep so, too, do you care for me. I find great security and safety in your monumental presence. When disorientation comes and knocks me off my feet, cause me to stand and regain my sense of awareness of your steadfast presence. Help me to find a way to reorient my life to you, to walk through the broken places, and to find the steadiness that can only be found through the indwelling presence of your Holy Spirit.

Calm my soul, O God, for you are my shepherd and I shall not want. To God be the glory now and forever. Amen.

DAY 38

Stillness and Peace

Scripture: Mark 4:35–40

> 35 On that day, when evening had come, [Jesus] said
> to [his disciples], "Let us go across to the other side."
> 36 And leaving the crowd, they took him with them in
> the boat, just as he was. And other boats were with him.
> 37 And a great windstorm arose, and the waves were break-
> ing into the boat, so that the boat was already filling.
> 38 But he was in the stern, asleep on the cushion. And
> they woke him and said to him, "Teacher, do you
> not care that we are perishing?" 39 And he awoke and
> rebuked the wind and said to the sea, "Peace! Be still!"
> And the wind ceased, and there was a great calm.
> 40 He said to them, "Why are you so afraid? Have you still
> no faith?"

Psalm 46:10

> Be still, and know that I am God.

Devotional Thoughts: Jesus asks his disciples, "Where is your faith?" Just as the disciples had no answer, we often have no answer to that question either. Where is our faith? Is it gone? Or possibly, we have a faith that cannot handle the hard parts of life. We also become lost in the intensity of traumatic experiences and we cannot seem to find our way out. Other times, we are so traumatized that the act of trusting anyone or anything is beyond our capability. God calls to us, at these times, to enter a deeper relationship with him, to find a new orientation.

When we have lost our capacity to trust anyone, we can look to Jesus' response in this story. "Peace" is what he first offers. This concept of "peace" often seems unattainable to traumatized people. Peace is nonexistent in our days and our nights. Yet, Jesus' first offering to this mighty storm is "peace." He provides us with peace through prayer, scripture reading, church attendance, and people around us. We also can receive peace through the beauty of nature and of quiet time with God. However, peace is a process for the highly traumatized. Peace requires trust and trust often is beyond the abilities of the traumatized.

Learning to trust again is a necessity for people who want to heal from their trauma. Traumatic happenings in our lives teach us that life is not fair and not everyone is trustworthy. Our God, however, is always trustworthy. He will not "perform" in the way that we request, but he is always with us and his love for us is unquestionable. The storms in our lives, however, cause us to question God. Jesus provides us a beginning in reorienting our trust in God.

Jesus' next words, "Be still" are ones that are difficult for traumatized people. Thoughts, memories, and terror can invade our waking and our sleeping lives. The instructions to "be still" can be the hardest command to follow as the continual cascade of fear, memories, and trauma fills our minds, emotions, and spirits. Being still requires us to trust God, to open ourselves to him.

Being still before God means that we open our spirits—our woundedness—to him. We have to calm the raging storms within our spirits and approach God with a stillness in our spirits. He then can begin to minister to us.

In the midst of these storms, be still. Calm your mind, your spirit, and your life. "Be still, and know that I am God" is a command that, even in the midst of powerful storms of trauma, we can find our way to the peace that comes from God.

Meditation: "Be still, and know that I am God." (Psalm 46:10)

Application: Choose a quiet time of day and be still before God. Open the self-protective covering with which you protect your spirit and sit in God's presence for one minute. Then lengthen the time slowly as the weeks pass. Be still and know that God is God. Through this experience, you will gradually come to feel his presence of peace calming the storm in your spirit.

Prayer: O Lord, I trust you with all my heart, but sometimes I wonder if you are there. It seems the winds are gusting and are threatening to blow everything away. I feel as if I am about to be carried away by these storms.

Arise, O Lord, and cause the winds to be still. Cause me to have complete confidence in your abilities to deliver me out of the storm's fury. As you delivered your disciples in the midst of the tempest, deliver me, Lord. I need you now, most Holy One. Know that I trust in you, even as I cry out to you in anguish. In this moment, cause me to trust you more and to know that you have already delivered me and given me healing, health, and peace of mind. To you I give thanks and praise forevermore. In Jesus' name I pray. Amen.

DAY 39

A New Creation

Scripture: II Corinthians 5:17

> [17] Therefore, if anyone is in Christ, he is a new creation. The old has passed away; behold, the new has come.

Devotional Thoughts: At the turn of the century, we were completing our fourth year at Naval Air Station Keflavik, Iceland. On our last New Year's Eve in Iceland, we waited to greet a new year and a new century. That night, a powerful winter storm was blasting the island and we feared that the normal New Year's Eve fireworks would be cancelled. Traditionally, all the towns around the bay between Keflavik and Reykjavik had fireworks each New Year's Eve.

Our family bundled up and went out to wait for the fireworks. When we exited the building, the frigid wind blasted us. The snow pelted us and the kids turned their backs to the wind, trying to avoid being blown over. As we moved out from the cover of the building, we had to hold the younger two because the wind was so strong. They could not walk or even stand against it. The storm blew fiercely and the time for the fireworks passed.

Suddenly the snow stopped and we spotted the fireworks exploding around the peninsula. We could momentarily even see around to Reykjavik for their fireworks. Then the snow began again and we huddled together.

We commented on what an awesome way to welcome a new century with the fireworks exploding and the wind and snow showing the power of God. Suddenly, the snow stopped again and the clouds parted above us.

Standing in a field of snow overlooking the town below, we looked up at the sky and saw the most awesome display of northern lights that we had ever seen. The sky crawled with blue-green fingers that joined together and parted in a graceful dance between the clouds.

Just as suddenly, the clouds closed and we were again pelted with snow. The kids took cover in our coats until they heard the fireworks. They peeked out and watched them exploding in town. Then the snow stopped and the northern lights again appeared, dancing across the sky.

We watched in fascination as the colors formed intricate patterns in the sky. The fireworks around the bay were nothing compared to this mighty show. Then the clouds closed and the snow again pelted us.

This pattern continued for almost two hours. Though we were freezing in the bitter cold, no one wanted to go inside. The fireworks shows were especially long as the new century was welcomed into this cold, dark land.

The northern lights that we watched reminded us all of the power of God over our world. We stayed out in the cold until we were sure that the clouds would not open again. We welcomed a new century that night with people in a distant land. We welcomed a new century with God's mighty show of power that reminded us that he is in control of all that is.

We realized that the old had indeed passed away and the new had come in power and glory. Who we were does not determine who we are and who we will be in God's eyes. He has the power to create in us newness, no matter how we feel about ourselves. God creates us anew through his Son, Jesus.

As we wait out the storms in our lives, we can be assured that God will create newness for us. When we feel that we are in a distant land and removed from what we once knew, God will provide an awesome show of his power and strength. God's show of his power and love can be beyond anything that we have ever experienced. Look for the new that God will bring to you.

Meditation: "The old has passed away; behold, the new has come." (II Corinthians 5:17b)

Application: How have you experienced the power of God? When have you experienced "old" passing away and "new" coming? Ask God to create in you a new heart. Ask God to help you put the "old" behind and to embrace the new.

Prayer: Father, you have reminded me many times that you have made me to be a new creation. You have encouraged me to put off the old and to be wrapped in this newness. As I stand and gaze at the wonder of your creation, the beauty of your faithfulness shines in the brightness of the dark night. Cause me to walk in the fullness of the new creation that you have made me.

Today, O Lord, the old has gone and the new has come forth. New confidence, new growth, and new faith are among the gifts you have bestowed on me. I find that I have an ever-increasing love for you as I journey closer and closer to you. Thank you forever, Lord, for your steadfast love and for the work you have done in me. In you, Lord Jesus, be praise and glory forever. Amen.

DAY 40

Peace

Scripture: John 14:27

> 27 Peace I leave with you; my peace I give to you. Not as the world gives do I give to you. Let not your hearts be troubled, neither let them be afraid.

Devotional Thoughts: At the time that Jesus said these words, Jesus and his disciples had completed what we now call Jesus' last supper. Jesus began talking with his disciples, explaining what was about to happen to him and providing them with comfort as he could.

This powerful verse speaks to us when our minds are chaotic, our nights are terror-filled, and our days are oppressive. It provides a promise of peace when we are in times of disorientation. "Peace" is the focus of Jesus' comforting words to his disciples. He leaves peace with them. He gives us the same peace today.

The peace of which Jesus speaks is not the peace about which we usually think. We often think of peace as the absence of fighting and discord. Peace can be the absence of recurring nightmares. Peace can be a small respite from the chaos that runs rampant through our minds. Peace can provide a safe haven when we are filled with fear.

This peace—Jesus' peace—is one that addresses our spiritual trauma. Jesus' peace can slowly creep into our spirits, loosening the bonds of anxiety and anger. His peace can bring relief from the trauma's effects with which we have lived for years.

Jesus' encouragement to us as well as his disciples is for us not to let our hearts be troubled. The chaos and horror that replay in our minds and spirits bring a troubled spirit to us. Jesus' peace can offset that troubled spirit. This peace can calm our weary spirits. Jesus instructs us to avoid letting our "hearts be troubled" which means to avoid allowing ourselves to be anxious. He will care for us.

Jesus also instructs his disciples not to be afraid. The fears that nightmares or flashbacks produce and the shame and guilt that memories produce should be what we try to avoid. Too often, though, we are trapped in these memories and feelings. Jesus promises peace to us. The peace that Jesus promises can overcome our fears, memories, and terrors. This peace fills us with hope in the resurrected Jesus. This hope brings healing through the Holy Spirit.

We find that as we move from a state of disorientation to a new orientation, we begin to understand at a deeper level the workings of God in our lives and on the earth. We find that our traumatized spirit can find peace and hope through the Holy Spirit. In our new orientation, we can bask in the love of God as our soul is filled with peace and love.

Then, each time the nightmares return, each time the chaos begins to reign, each time we feel frightened, we can turn to Jesus and he will comfort us. He will heal us and he will soothe our weary souls.

Ask God to provide you with the peace that Jesus promises us. Open your heart, mind, and spirit to the healing power of God our Father, Jesus his Son, and the Holy Spirit. Through God's healing, we find a new orientation that provides us with hope.

Meditation: [Jesus said], "Let not your hearts be troubled, neither let them be afraid." (John 14:27b)

Application: Pray for God to provide you with Jesus' peace. Calm your spirit and mind. Ask God to show you the way to live in this peace. Ask God to show you the path to hope.

Prayer: Eternal Father, it is in your divine care that I find peace. A peace that brings hope and new life. A peace that comforts and soothes the brokenhearted. A peace that empowers and lifts up. A peace that changes lives for all of eternity!

Thank you, Father, for reopening my heart, mind, and spirit through the healing that can only come from you. In your presence, I have experienced a new orientation that fills me with awe and wonder. As you have freed me from the past, you have opened the door to hope in the future. A hope that is filled with your love and peace.

In these days ahead, continue to be my strength. Walk with me. Allow me, through your Spirit, to be the person you have created me to be: healed, reconciled, and committed to you forevermore. In the holy name of Jesus Christ I pray. Amen.

Epilogue

Forty days does not seem long enough to journey through all of the chaos that can be trapped in the minds of the traumatized. When we view "forty days" as a symbol of a journey, however, the movement from despair to hope becomes possible. The journey can be one that takes years if the traumatization is severe; yet we know that we can trust God to lead us on the journey. We can trust that the Holy Spirit will come alongside us to comfort us as we move deeper into God's love.

As you take this journey, may you come to know the God of love and comfort. May you seek his guidance as you move into the depths of your woundedness. And may you be certain of his presence accompanying you throughout your life.

Recently, we became aware of a song by Zach Williams and Dolly Parton. This song applies to wounded and traumatized people. It is our story, and it can be your story. The song reflects the struggles of the traumatized who no longer relate to family and friends. They experience their world as crashing in and their path as one of loneliness. Many of the stories within this devotional reflect this perspective.

The hope that we have through our faith, however, is reflected in the words of this song. Looking back, we can see that Jesus has been, is now, and will always be in all of our life's broken pieces. It is from this promise of presence that we find hope within our traumatic experiences. We cannot make it on our own, but Jesus is there whether we are aware of him or not.

We are often waiting, searching, and hurting before we find healing. It is only when we look back on these hard times that we see Jesus' presence in our lives. It is the blessing buried in the broken pieces of our lives.

There Was Jesus

Every time I tried to make it on my own
Every time I tried to stand and start to fall
And all those lonely roads that I have travelled on
There was Jesus

When the life I built came crashing to the ground
When the friends I had were nowhere to be found
I couldn't see it then, but I can see it now
There was Jesus

In the waiting, in the searching
In the healing and the hurting
Like a blessing buried in the broken pieces
Every minute, every moment
Where I've been and where I'm going
Even when I didn't know it or couldn't see it
There was Jesus

For this man who needs amazing kind of grace
For forgiveness at a price I couldn't pay
I'm not perfect so I thank God every day
There was Jesus

In the waiting, in the searching
In the healing and the hurting
Like a blessing buried in the broken pieces
Every minute, every moment

Where I've been and where I'm going
Even when I didn't know it or couldn't see it
There was Jesus

On the mountain, in the valleys
In the shadows of the alleys
In the fire, in the flood
Always is and always was
No I never walk alone
You are always there

In the waiting, in the searching
In the healing and the hurting
Like a blessing buried in the broken pieces
Every minute, every moment
Where I've been and where I'm going
Even when I didn't know it or couldn't see it
There was Jesus. (Williams and Parton, 2019)

As people who need an amazing kind of grace, may you find the blessings from God buried in the broken pieces. You do not have to walk alone because Jesus is with you wherever you are going…even when you do not know it or cannot see it. There is Jesus. We encourage you to begin your journey out of dcspair so that your spirit can find peace and hope in this life.

We never walk alone.

A Benediction of Hope

The LORD bless you and keep you;
the LORD make his face to shine upon you and be gracious to you;
the LORD lift up his countenance upon you and give you peace.
Numbers 6:24–26

References

Brueggemann, W. *Spirituality of the Psalms.* Minneapolis, MN: Fortress Press, 2002.

De Gruchy, J. ed., *Dietrich Bonhoeffer: Witness to Jesus Christ.* Minneapolis, MN: Fortress Press, 1991.

Grant, R. *The Way of the Wound: A Spirituality of Trauma and Transformation.* Self-published, 1996.

Heartley, L. P. *The Go-Between.* New York: The New York Review of Books, 1953.

Hoge, C. W. *Once a warrior Always a Warrior: Navigating the Transition from Combat to Home—Including Combat Stress, PTSD, and TBI.* Guilford, CT: Lyons, 2010.

Lincoln, A. (2002). Transcript of Gettysburg Address (1863). https://www.ourdocuments.gov/doc.php?flash=true&doc=36&page=transcript.

Marlantes, K. *What it is Like to Go to War.* New York: Grove, 2011.

Meadors, P. & Lamson, A. "Compassion Fatigue and Secondary Traumatization: Provider Self Care on Intensive Care Units for Children." *Journal of Pediatric Health Care,* 22:1 (2008), 24–34.

Oswald Chambers quotes. (2016). https://www.goodreads.com/author/quotes/41469.Oswald_Chambers?page=3.

Stott, John. *Your Confirmation: A Christian Handbook for Adults.* N.d. http://www.stpl.ca/Resources/Confirmation/Stott8.pdf.

Williams, Z., & Parton, D. "There Was Jesus." *Rescue Story* [Album]. Essential Music Publishing, 2019.

Biographies

Captain Michael W. Langston, CHC, USN, retired from 36 years of service (30 active) in the U. S. Marine Corps (infantry officer) and the U. S. Navy Chaplain Corps. Receiving a diagnosis of severe PTSD after his tours in Afghanistan and Iraq, CAPT Langston continued on active duty as the Commanding Officer for the Naval Chaplaincy School and Center. His military awards include the Legion of Merit, Bronze Star, and the Defense Meritorious Service Medal. A native of Alabama, CAPT Langston grew up in Lafayette, LA, where he played football for the University of Louisiana in Lafayette. CAPT Langston's educational degrees include: Doctor of Philosophy (University of Aberdeen), Doctor of Ministry, Master of Arts in National Strategy and Strategic Affairs (Naval War College), Master of Divinity, and Bachelor of Science (Physical Education). He is Professor of Practical Theology and Chaplaincy in Columbia Biblical Seminary at Columbia International University.

Kathy J. Langston, PhD, teaches professional communication at the University of South Carolina. A native of Greenville, South Carolina, Dr. Langston embraced military spouse life and enjoyed her ministry with Navy and Marine Corps spouses. Dr. Langston taught university religion and English courses to military students for over fifteen years. Her degrees include: Doctor of Philosophy in English (Composition and Rhetoric), Master of Arts (English—Professional and Technical Writing), Master of Divinity (Languages), and Bachelor of Arts (English). The Langstons have three children, two daughters-in-law, and three grandchildren. The Langstons have been married over thirty-seven years.

Visit the Langstons at their website:
HopeThruFaith.com
Twitter: @HopeThruFaith
Facebook: HopeThruFaith